Pre-Work for
Freed-Up Financial Living

IMPORTANT
Please read and complete all pre-work prior to beginning the course.

Dear *Freed-Up Financial Living* Participant,

We're delighted that you have decided to participate in the *Freed-Up Financial Living* course from the Good $ense Ministry!

Course Goal

The goal of this course is for you to become grounded in a biblical understanding of a proper relationship to money and possessions and to commit to and begin developing a biblically-based Spending Plan.

By the end of the course, you will have the first draft of a usable Spending Plan in your hand, the knowledge in your head to implement it, and a commitment in your heart to follow through on it. The Good $ense Ministry is committed to providing you with the principles, practical steps, and individual assistance to help make that happen.

Pre-Work

In order for the course to be as valuable and productive as possible, it is very important to complete the pre-work prior to beginning the course. Completing the forms may take several hours so it is advisable to begin as soon as you receive these materials. The information you are asked to collect is confidential, and no one else will see it. Throughout the course, you will use your pre-work information to establish your personal Spending Plan.

Supplies

In addition to your completed pre-work, please make sure you have a couple of pencils, an eraser, and a pocket calculator when you begin the course.

Prayer

We pray that this experience will be a valuable one for you and that you will grow in your understanding of biblical financial principles and your ability to put them into practice.

The Good $ense Team

Pre-Work Instructions

Seven forms are included in the pre-work to help you prepare for *Freed-Up Financial Living*. Please allow plenty of time prior to the course to gather the information and to complete each form. Instructions to help you complete each form are listed below.

Goals to Achieve this Year

Make it a priority to reflect on your financial goals. If you are married, make time to discuss financial goals with your spouse. These goals will become the basis for shaping your Spending Plan, and they will provide motivation for following through on your decisions in the months ahead.

What I Owe

As you fill out the second column (Amount) of this section, use the total balance due on each item.

What I Own

This section is optional, but we encourage you to fill it out so you can calculate a simplified version of your net worth. Consider the value of things you own to be the amount you would expect to get if you sold the items.

Gift List

Here's an often overlooked or underestimated part of spending. Write the names of individuals you will be purchasing gifts for in the coming year. Remember to include cards, postage at Christmas, parties, etc. You may wish to include some money for as-yet-unannounced weddings, etc.

What I Spend

Gather as much information as you can to determine a monthly average for expenses in each category. Going through your checkbook and your credit card bills for the past year will probably be helpful. Be sure to include periodic expense items such as auto insurance, taxes, etc., that may not be paid on a monthly basis. If you have not kept records in the past, some of the categories may be difficult to estimate. Give it your best shot, recognizing that if you don't have records showing how much you're spending in a particular area, the amount is probably more than you think it is!

The income figures at the top of the page should be your monthly take-home pay after taxes and other deductions. Make a note of any deductions (such as medical insurance, retirement contributions, etc). Where those items occur under expenses, enter the notation "payroll deduction."

If your income varies from month to month, use a *conservative* monthly estimate based on the last two or three years' earnings. Referring back to your income tax records could be helpful in making this determination. Remember, you are looking for after-tax, take-home income.

Money Motivation Quiz

This exercise will provide insightful information on your behavior regarding money. If you are married, two copies of the quiz are provided so you and your spouse can both take the quiz. Explanations are included on the back of the quiz. No peeking before you answer the questions!

Money Autobiography

This is an optional exercise that can also provide insight into why we handle money as we do. All of us have been influenced by how money was handled in our homes growing up — sometimes for better, sometimes for worse. Reflecting on the questions asked in the Money Autobiography can raise our consciousness of those influences and help us take steps to counteract any that may have been negative.

Goals to Achieve this Year

Please allow adequate time to give serious consideration to your goals. Carefully-considered, realistic goals that flow out of what's really important to you are powerful motivators. That motivation will be very helpful to you in following through on the steps necessary to achieve your goals and ultimately, financial freedom!

Overall Goal

State your overall goal in attending *Freed-Up Financial Living*. What do you hope will happen as a result?

My Goal:

Specific Goals to Achieve

Following are some possible goals that can serve as "thought starters" for you. The important thing is that the goals you list are ones that are truly important to you. Be as specific as you can, using dates, amounts, etc.

Pay off debt: *Mortgage & Home Equity*

Save for: *Retirement / Emergencies*
(major purchase, replacement items, college, retirement)

Increase my giving to: *My church / Missions*

Become more disciplined in: *Spiritual Life*

Other: *Spending*

Other: *Self-Discipline*

Other:

What I Own (optional)

I Own (Assets)	Amount
Checking Account	680.⁰⁰
Savings Account	127.⁰⁰
Other Savings	
Insurance (cash value)	
Retirement	9,500.⁰⁰
Home (market value)	230,000.⁰⁰
Auto (market value)	6000.⁰⁰
Second Auto (market value)	1750.⁰⁰
Bass Boat	5000⁰⁰
Money Owed to Me	
Other *Lawn Equip*	4150.⁰⁰
Other *Snow Blower*	600.⁰⁰
Total of All I Own	257,807.⁰⁰

What I Owe

I Owe (Liabilities)	Amount	Minimum Monthly Payments	Interest Percentage
Mortgage (current balance)	40,968.⁰⁰	579.³⁵	5.99%
Home Equity Loans	99,350.⁰⁰	280.⁰⁰	3.25%
Credit Cards *Menards*	2191.⁰⁰	57.⁰⁰	24.9% annual
J.C. Penney	445.⁰⁰	32.⁰⁰	26.99
Car Loans	0	0	0
Education Loans	0	0	0
Family/Friends	0	0	0
Other *Back Taxes*	750.⁰⁰		
Total of All I Owe	143,904.⁰⁰		

Net Worth (optional)

Total of All I Own − Total of All I Owe = Net Worth (in earthly terms, not God's!)*

_____ − _____ = _____

*Never confuse your self-worth with your net worth. In God's eyes each one of us is of infinite worth.

Gift List

List the names of those for whom you buy gifts and the amounts you typically spend on each occasion.*

Name	Birthday	Christmas	Anniversary	Other
1. Tom	50⁰⁰	100⁰⁰	50⁰⁰	
2. Cathy	50⁰⁰	100⁰⁰	50⁰⁰	
3. Jennifer	30⁰⁰	30⁰⁰		
4. Dan	30⁰⁰	30⁰⁰		
5. Sophia	30⁰⁰	30⁰⁰		
6. Jason	30⁰⁰	30⁰⁰		
7. Abby	30⁰⁰	30⁰⁰		
8. Nevaeh	30⁰⁰	30⁰⁰		
9.	30⁰⁰	30⁰⁰		
10. Justin	30⁰⁰	30⁰⁰		
11. Sally	30⁰⁰	20⁰⁰		
12. Pastor	0	20⁰⁰		
13. Wife	0	20⁰⁰		
14.				
15.				
16.				
17.				
18.				
19.				
20.				
Total	370.⁰⁰	510⁰⁰	100,⁰⁰	

Grand Total (of all columns) $ 980⁰⁰

Monthly Average (Total ÷ 12) = $ 82.⁰⁰

*You may wish to also include the cost of holiday decorations, entertaining, etc.

What I Spend

Earnings/Income Per Month	Totals
Salary #1 (net take-home)	445.⁰⁰/wk. #1928.³³/mo.
Salary #2 (net take-home)	60.⁰⁰/wk. 240.⁰⁰/mo.
Other (less taxes)	700.⁰⁰/mo rent
Total Monthly Income	$ 2868.³³

% Guide*

1. Giving		$ 246.⁶⁶
Church	50.⁰⁰/wk 216.⁶⁶/mo.	
Other Contributions	30.⁰⁰/mo	
2. Savings	**15%**	**$ 216.⁶⁶**
Emergency	20.⁰⁰	
Replacement	20.⁰⁰ } 216.⁶⁶/mo.	
Long Term	10.⁰⁰	
3. Debt	**0-10%**	**$ 369.⁰⁰**

Credit Cards:

Visa	
MasterCard	
Discover ~~American Express~~ Menard's	#2191.⁰⁰/57.⁰⁰/mo.
Gas Cards	
Department Stores	675.⁰⁰/32.⁰⁰/mo.
Education Loans	

Other Loans:

Bank Loans Home Equity	99350.⁰⁰/280.⁰⁰/mo.
Credit Union	
Family/Friends	
Other	

4. Housing	**25-36%**	**$ 1176.⁶⁰**
Mortgage/Taxes/Rent	#40,968.⁰⁰/579.³⁵/mo.	
Maintenance/Repairs		

Utilities:

Electric	119.⁴⁵/mo.
Gas	205.⁰⁰/mo.
Water	⊘
Trash	180.⁰⁰/yr. #15.⁰⁰/mo
Telephone/Internet	87.⁰⁰/mo.
Cable TV	52.⁴⁰/mo.
Other (Land Taxes)	1,300.⁰⁰/108.³³/mo

5. Auto/Transp.	**15-20%**	**$ 191.⁹¹**
Car Payments/License	143.⁰⁰/yr. 11.⁹¹/mo.	
Gas & Bus/Train/Parking	160.⁰⁰/mo.	
Oil/Lube/Maintenance	20.⁰⁰/mo.	

6. Insurance (Paid by you)	**5%**	**$ 274.⁸⁶**
Auto	77.⁴²/mo	
Homeowners	197.44/mo.	
Life		
Medical/Dental		
Other		

7. Household/Personal	**15-25%**	**$ 672.⁰⁰**
Groceries	400.⁰⁰/mo	
Clothes/Dry Cleaning	25.⁰⁰/mo.	
Gifts	82.⁰⁰/mo	
Household Items		

Personal:

Tobacco & Alcohol	⊘
Cosmetics	#5/mo.
Barber/Beauty	#20/mo.

Other:

Books/Magazines/Music	30.⁰⁰/mo.
Allowances	80.⁰⁰/mo.
Personal Technology	
Extracurricular Activities	10.⁰⁰/mo
Education	
Pets	20.⁰⁰/mo.
Miscellaneous	

8. Entertainment	**5-10%**	**$ 253.³³**

Going Out:

Meals	#150.⁰⁰/mo.
Movies/Events	#10/mo.
Babysitting	⊘
Travel (Vacation/Trips)	#1,000.⁰⁰/yr. 83.³³/mo.

Other:

Fitness/Sports	
Hobbies	10.⁰⁰/mo.
Media Rental	
Other	

9. Prof. Services	**5-15%**	**$ 100.⁰⁰**
Child Care	⊘	
Medical/Dental/Prescriptions	100.⁰⁰/mo	

Other:

Legal	
Counseling	
Professional Dues	

10. Misc. Small Cash Expenditures	**2-3%**	**$ _____**
Total Expenses		$ _____

*This is a percent of total monthly income. These are guidelines only and may be different for individual situations. However, there should be good rationale for a significant variance.

TOTAL MONTHLY INCOME	$ 2868
LESS TOTAL EXPENSES	$ 3500.
INCOME OVER/(UNDER) EXPENSES	$ ⟨632⟩

Money Motivation Quiz

For each of the questions below, circle the letter that best describes your response.

1. Money is important because it allows me to…
   a. Do what I want to do.
   b. Feel secure. *(circled)*
   c. Get ahead in life.
   d. Buy things for others.

2. I feel that money…
   a. Frees up my time.
   b. Can solve my problems.
   c. Is a means to an end. *(circled)*
   d. Helps make relationships smoother.

3. When it comes to saving money, I…
   a. Don't have a plan and rarely save. *(circled)*
   b. Have a plan and stick to it.
   c. Don't have a plan but manage to save anyway.
   d. Don't make enough money to save.

4. If someone asks about my personal finances, I…
   a. Feel defensive.
   b. Realize I need more education and information.
   c. Feel comfortable and competent.
   d. Would rather talk about something else. *(circled)*

5. When I make a major purchase, I…
   a. Go with what my intuition tells me.
   b. Research a great deal before buying.
   c. Feel I'm in charge – it's my/our money.
   d. Ask friends/family first. *(circled)*

6. If I have money left over at the end of the month, I…
   a. Go out and have a good time.
   b. Put the money into savings. *(circled)*
   c. Look for a good investment.
   d. Buy a gift for someone.

7. If I discover I paid more for something than a friend did, I…
   a. Couldn't care less.
   b. Feel it's OK because I also find bargains at times.
   c. Assume they spent more time shopping, and time is money.
   d. Feel upset and angry at myself. *(circled)*

8. When paying bills, I…
   a. Put it off and sometimes forget.
   b. Pay them when due, but no sooner. *(circled)*
   c. Pay when I get to it, but don't want to be hassled.
   d. Worry that my credit will suffer if I miss a payment.

9. When it comes to borrowing money, I…
   a. Simply won't/don't like to feel indebted.
   b. Only borrow as a last resort.
   c. Tend to borrow from banks or other business sources. *(circled)*
   d. Ask friends and family because they know I'll pay.

10. When eating out with friends, I prefer to…
    a. Divide the bill proportionately.
    b. Ask for separate checks. *(circled)*
    c. Charge the bill to my credit/debit card and have others pay me.
    d. Pay the entire bill because I like to treat my friends.

11. When it comes to tipping, I…
    a. Sometimes do and sometimes don't.
    b. Just call me Scrooge.
    c. Resent it, but always tip the right amount.
    d. Tip generously because I like to be well thought of. *(circled)*

12. If I suddenly came into a lot of money, I…
    a. Wouldn't have to work.
    b. Wouldn't have to worry about the future.
    c. Could really build up my business.
    d. Would spend a lot on family and friends and enjoy time with them more. *(circled)*

13. When indecisive about a purchase, I often tell myself…
    a. It's only money.
    b. It's a bargain. *(circled)*
    c. It's a good investment.
    d. He/she will love it.

14. In our family…
    a. I do/will handle all the money and pay all the bills. *(circled)*
    b. My partner does/will take care of the finances.
    c. I do/will pay my bills and my partner will do the same.
    d. We do/will sit down together to pay bills.

Score: Tally your answers by the number of times you chose each letter.

a. 2   c. 1
b. 5   d. 5

To understand your results, see the explanation on the back of this page.

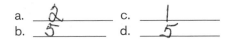

Understanding the Results of Your Money Motivation Quiz

Money means different things to different people based on a variety of factors, such as temperament and life experiences. Often the meaning of money and the way it motivates us is subtle and something we are not always aware of.

This simple quiz is designed to give you an indication of how strongly you are influenced by the following money motivations: Freedom, Security, Power, and Love. None are inherently good or bad, although each certainly has its dark side.

The key to your money motivation is reflected in the relative number of a, b, c, or d answers.

"A" answers indicate that money relates to **Freedom**. To you, money means having the freedom to do what you like.

"B" answers indicate that money relates to **Security**. You need to feel safe and secure, and you desire the stability and protection that money supposedly provides.

"C" answers indicate that money relates to **Power**. Personal success and control are important to you, and you appreciate the power money sometimes provides.

"D" answers indicate that money relates to **Love**. You like to use money to express love and build relationships.

One of the keys to managing money wisely is to understand our relationship to it. We hope this exercise gives you some helpful insights. You may wish to share your scores with your spouse or a friend and discuss whether their perceptions of your money motivations are consistent with your scores.

Money Motivation Quiz

Directions

For each of the questions below, circle the letter that best describes your response.

1. Money is important because it allows me to…
   a. Do what I want to do.
   b. Feel secure.
   c. Get ahead in life.
   d. Buy things for others.

2. I feel that money…
   a. Frees up my time.
   b. Can solve my problems.
   c. Is a means to an end.
   d. Helps make relationships smoother.

3. When it comes to saving money, I…
   a. Don't have a plan and rarely save.
   b. Have a plan and stick to it.
   c. Don't have a plan but manage to save anyway.
   d. Don't make enough money to save.

4. If someone asks about my personal finances, I…
   a. Feel defensive.
   b. Realize I need more education and information.
   c. Feel comfortable and competent.
   d. Would rather talk about something else.

5. When I make a major purchase, I…
   a. Go with what my intuition tells me.
   b. Research a great deal before buying.
   c. Feel I'm in charge – it's my/our money.
   d. Ask friends/family first.

6. If I have money left over at the end of the month, I…
   a. Go out and have a good time.
   b. Put the money into savings.
   c. Look for a good investment.
   d. Buy a gift for someone.

7. If I discover I paid more for something than a friend did, I…
   a. Couldn't care less.
   b. Feel it's OK because I also find bargains at times.
   c. Assume they spent more time shopping, and time is money.
   d. Feel upset and angry at myself.

8. When paying bills, I…
   a. Put it off and sometimes forget.
   b. Pay them when due, but no sooner.
   c. Pay when I get to it, but don't want to be hassled.
   d. Worry that my credit will suffer if I miss a payment.

9. When it comes to borrowing money, I…
   a. Simply won't/don't like to feel indebted.
   b. Only borrow as a last resort.
   c. Tend to borrow from banks or other business sources.
   d. Ask friends and family because they know I'll pay.

10. When eating out with friends, I prefer to…
    a. Divide the bill proportionately.
    b. Ask for separate checks.
    c. Charge the bill to my credit/debit card and have others pay me.
    d. Pay the entire bill because I like to treat my friends.

11. When it comes to tipping, I…
    a. Sometimes do and sometimes don't.
    b. Just call me Scrooge.
    c. Resent it, but always tip the right amount.
    d. Tip generously because I like to be well thought of.

12. If I suddenly came into a lot of money, I…
    a. Wouldn't have to work.
    b. Wouldn't have to worry about the future.
    c. Could really build up my business.
    d. Would spend a lot on family and friends and enjoy time with them more.

13. When indecisive about a purchase, I often tell myself…
    a. It's only money.
    b. It's a bargain.
    c. It's a good investment.
    d. He/she will love it.

14. In our family…
    a. I do/will handle all the money and pay all the bills.
    b. My partner does/will take care of the finances.
    c. I do/will pay my bills and my partner will do the same.
    d. We do/will sit down together to pay bills.

Score: Tally your answers by the number of times you chose each letter.

a. ___3___   c. ___2___
b. ___6___   d. ___2___

To understand your results, see the explanation on the back of this page.

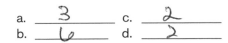

Understanding the Results of Your Money Motivation Quiz

Money means different things to different people based on a variety of factors, such as temperament and life experiences. Often the meaning of money and the way it motivates us is subtle and something we are not always aware of.

This simple quiz is designed to give you an indication of how strongly you are influenced by the following money motivations: Freedom, Security, Power, and Love. None are inherently good or bad, although each certainly has its dark side.

The key to your money motivation is reflected in the relative number of a, b, c, or d answers.

"A" answers indicate that money relates to **Freedom**. To you, money means having the freedom to do what you like.

"B" answers indicate that money relates to **Security**. You need to feel safe and secure, and you desire the stability and protection that money supposedly provides.

"C" answers indicate that money relates to **Power**. Personal success and control are important to you, and you appreciate the power money sometimes provides.

"D" answers indicate that money relates to **Love**. You like to use money to express love and build relationships.

One of the keys to managing money wisely is to understand our relationship to it. We hope this exercise gives you some helpful insights. You may wish to share your scores with your spouse or a friend and discuss whether their perceptions of your money motivations are consistent with your scores.

Money Autobiography

If we added up all the hours we spend making money, spending money, worrying about money, fighting over money, and trying to protect our money, we might find that a majority of our waking hours are spent on this subject. Jesus spent a significant amount of his teaching time on the subject of money and our relationship to it. It is a big and important aspect of life.

Often how we relate to our money and possessions is heavily influenced, positively or negatively, by our early life experiences and how money was handled in the households we grew up in. Taking time to reflect upon the following questions can make us aware of those influences and allow us to take steps to change any negative behaviors they may have fostered.

Personal History
1. What one word or phrase would you use to describe your life with money?
2. What are some of your earliest memories of money?
3. Growing up, did you feel rich, poor, or neither?
4. What is the first money you recall earning, and how did you earn it? How did you spend it?

Family History
1. Who were your money management role models?
2. Who handled the money in your family?
3. How did they handle the money?
4. Was money discussed in your family?
5. Was money abundant or scarce?
6. How did your family discuss and express generosity?

Present Family
1. Who are your current money management role models?
2. Who handles the money?
3. How do they handle the money?
4. Is money easily discussed?
5. Is money abundant or scarce?
6. How does your family discuss and express generosity?

Current Financial Realities
1. How much money has passed through my hands in the last 10 years? 20 years?
2. How much money do I anticipate will pass through my hands in the next 10 years? 20 years?

Material adapted from *The Whys and Hows of Money Leadership: A Curriculum for Pastors and Church Leaders* by Mark Vincent (with Michael Meier), Lead Partner, Design for Ministry, www.designforministry.com. Used by permission.

Pre-Work

GOOD $ENSE
CORE CURRICULUM

Freed-Up
financial living

How to Get There Using Biblical Principles

Freed-Up
financial living

How to Get There Using Biblical Principles

Participant's Workbook

Dick Towner and John Tofilon
With Shannon Plate

WILLOW
Willow Creek Resources

Freed-Up Financial Living Participant's Workbook
Copyright © 2008 by Willow Creek Association

Requests for information should be addressed to:
Willow Creek Association
67 E. Algonquin Road
South Barrington, IL 60010

ISBN: 0-744-19637-X

Cover design by CHANGEffect

Interior design by Rebecca Gallagher, 32 Design

Printed in the United States of America

09 10 11 12 13 14 • 10 9 8 7 6 5 4 3 2

Contents

Foreword

In school they tell us we're being equipped to earn it. Then for the rest of our lives — for as many as fifty or sixty hours a week — we're busy making it. We invest countless hours in thought and discussion deciding how to deal with it. We walk around shopping malls for hours on end determining how we're going to spend it. We're caught up more often than we'd like to admit worrying we won't have enough of it. We dream and scheme to figure out ways to acquire more of it.

Arguments over it are a leading cause for marital disintegration. Despair over losing it has even led to suicide. Passion for it causes much of society's crime. The absence of it causes many of society's nightmares. Some view it as the root of all evil, while others think of it as the means for great good.

One thing is clear: we cannot afford to ignore the reality of the importance of money.

Over the years at Willow Creek Community Church we've been committed to tackling every important issue that faces the people who attend — from nutrition to sexuality, from building character to deepening relationships, from discovering and adoring the identity of God to preparing for death and eternity. One topic, however, that we've learned we must address regularly and directly is the subject that Christians wrestle with almost every day — the issue of how we handle personal finances.

Thankfully, there's no shortage of information on this crucial matter in the Bible, and it provides the basis for the materials you're about to dive into. More than two thousand Scripture passages touch on the theme of money. Jesus spoke about it frequently. About two-thirds of Jesus' parables make reference to our use of financial resources. He once warned that "where your treasure is, there your heart will be also." He talked often about these matters because he understood what was at stake. He knew that, left to our own devices, this area would quickly become a source of pain and frustration — and sometimes bondage. Worse, he saw how easily our hearts would be led astray from pure devotion to God into areas of worry and even obsession over possessions. He wanted to protect us from these pitfalls and to show us the liberty that comes from following God fully in every area of life, including this one.

> > >

So get ready to join the ranks of thousands of people from our church and other churches who have received tangible help in this area through Good $ense. This vital ministry has been refined and proven over many years by my friend and trusted co-laborer, Dick Towner, along with his Good $ense Ministry team. I'm confident that in this newly revised, updated, and expanded resource you'll find fresh avenues to increased financial freedom and, along the way, grow a more grateful spirit and generous heart.

And as you and others from your congregation experience this, your church will be liberated so it can reflect more and more of that giving spirit and heart to the community around you, making it a magnet to people who are desperately looking for the kind of freedom, life, and love they see in you.

Bill Hybels
Founding and Senior Pastor
Willow Creek Community Church

Acknowledgments

In the *Good $ense Budget Course* that predated this resource, there appeared an extensive list of acknowledgments. It is upon the shoulders of those same people that we stand as this new resource comes to fruition.

Special new mention is appropriate, however, for Stephanie Oakley who served as Project Director for this endeavor and for the dedicated and gifted team of video, design, and support personnel who made the finished resource possible. It really does "take a village" to produce a quality resource. So deep thanks for your part to:

Dave Schwarz, Lucas Mroz, and the entire WCA Media team for their hard work on re-imagining the look of the content and bringing it to life.

April Kimura-Anderson for her tireless work as the Marketing Director for this project.

Greg Bowman and Nancy Raney for their leadership, vision, and belief in the power of this course to change people's hearts and lives.

And to all of the people who had a hand in this project, big and small – our deepest gratitude and thanks.

Our Hopes for You

Dear Participant:

We are so glad you've decided to participate in the Good $ense *Freed-Up Financial Living* course! Although we don't know what your financial situation is or what motivated you to sign up for the course, we do have deeply-held hopes for you.

We hope the *Freed-Up* course will be more than just a learning experience about spending plans, finances, and your relationship to money. We hope it will also be a time for you to reflect on your relationship to God. This often happens naturally because our relationship to money is closely correlated to our relationship to God.

We hope you leave the course more aware of how your financial behavior is influenced – many times subconsciously – by forces within our culture that may or may not be consistent with your values and goals.

We hope you will discover tools and develop skills that will enable you to manage and control your finances, rather than allowing your finances to manage and control you. Money is a powerful thing. If we fail to control it, it will control us, and money, rather than God's still small voice, will make many key life decisions for us – where we live, what jobs we take, who our friends are, and more. We want you to gain the skills to master your money so you can experience a freedom in Christ you may have never known before.

Finally, we hope you leave this course with a deep sense of confidence that – with God's help – you really can do it! We want you to leave with a Spending Plan in your hand, the knowledge in your head to implement it, and the desire and motivation in your heart to follow through on it.

We pray that all these hopes will be true for you.

Dick Towner, John Tofilon, and Shannon Plate

SESSION 1

Two Masters, One Servant

Introduction and Welcome

You Can Do It!

I can do everything through him who gives me strength.
Philippians 4:13

Our Relationship to Money

- Our relationship to money has an incredible amount to do with our relationship to God.

  - "There is no such thing as being right with God and being wrong with money." – Ben Patterson

  - Money can become our chief rival god.

    For where your treasure is, there your heart will be also.
    Matthew 6:21

    …You cannot serve both God and money.
    Matthew 6:24 (NLT)

    For the love of money is a root of all kinds of evil…
    1 Timothy 6:10

    This has eternal significance.

- Our relationship to money and possessions is at the heart of the macro issues facing our world today.

- Money is a powerful thing!

The Pull of the Culture

Notes: *About values and priorities*

Most people live on $2/day around world.
Advertising was born and consumer debt
soared and stuff makes us feel good.
1.5 billion credit cards in America.

❋ ❋ ❋ Activity: Reaction to *The Pull of the Culture*

1. Put a checkmark next to the myth in the list below that you think influences you the most.

   ❑ Things bring happiness.

   ❑ Debt is expected and unavoidable.

   ☒ A little more money will solve all my problems.

2. If you're in a group, introduce yourself to each other, and then share the cultural myth that influences you most and how it impacts you.

Cultural Myths

- Debt is expected and unavoidable.

- Things bring happiness. *Advertising tells us this.*

- A little more money will solve all my problems.

Course Overview

In this course, you will:

- Contrast what the culture says about money with what the Bible says about money.

- Develop personal Spending Plans.

- Begin to experience peace, joy, and freedom in your financial life. *Yes!*

The Mind and Heart of God

See p. 153 in the Appendix for a list of Scripture verses about money.

Three Core Truths

1. God created everything (Genesis 1:1).

2. God owns everything.

> *The earth is the LORD's, and everything in it, the world, and all who live in it.*
> Psalm 24:1

3. We are trustees, not owners.

> *Now it is required that those who have been given a trust must prove faithful.*
> 1 Corinthians 4:2

   ○ A trustee has no rights, only responsibilities.

   ○ In eternal terms, everything we possess belongs to God.

Two Masters, One Servant

▶ ▶ ▶ Video: *The Pearl of Great Price*

✱ ✱ ✱ Activity: Reaction to *The Pearl of Great Price*

Get back into your groups, if applicable, and discuss your reaction to the video and how this truth might impact you.

If you're not in a group, take some time to write down your reaction in the space below.

Notes: *Jesus, the Pearl of Great Price gives us everything we need to use so we need to share everything we have and remember that we don't own it, He does.*

✱ Individual Activity: Owner or Trustee?

Reflect on your own finances and possessions. Put an X on the continuum below to reflect how you see yourself, whether as an owner or a trustee.

I see myself as an owner.　　　*Much of the time* ✗　　　I see myself as a trustee.

The Pull of the Culture vs. the Mind and Heart of God

Foolish

Faithful

The Pull of the Culture

The Mind and Heart of God

Two Masters, One Servant

No one can serve two masters. For you will hate one and love the other; you will be devoted to one and despise the other. You cannot serve both God and money.
Matthew 6:24 (NLT)

…Well done, good and faithful servant!…
Matthew 25:21   *trustee*

Yes, a person is a fool to store up earthly wealth but not have a rich relationship with God.
Luke 12:21 (NLT)

Two Great Truths

1. (God holds us accountable) for how we manage the money and possessions entrusted to us.

2. We will be found either faithful or foolish.

> **Key Question:** Will God consider my financial decisions to be faithful or foolish?

⚙ Individual Activity: Faithful or Foolish?

Think about some of the financial decisions you've made over the last few days, whether large or small. Reflect for a few moments on whether God would consider them faithful or foolish, and write your thoughts in the space below.

My thoughts: *Mostly foolish but little $*

Five Financial Areas of Life

- Earning

- Giving – *Eternal*

- Saving – *Future*

- Debt – *Past*

- Spending *Current*

When we choose to be faithful in these five financial areas, Scripture indicates that we become a:

- Diligent Earner

- Generous Giver

- Wise Saver

- Cautious Debtor

- Prudent Spender

Financial Freedom

Financial Freedom: The contentment we feel as we faithfully manage our financial resources according to God's principles and purposes.

- The key word is "contentment."

- Being financially faithful leads to financial freedom.

- God honors our trust in His principles.

The Spending Plan

Budget: The fundamental tool that enables us to control our money so that it doesn't control us — a Spending Plan for how we will allocate our financial resources.

- A Spending Plan is a way to reach our financial goals and live out our values and priorities.

- Using a Spending Plan produces freedom!

    ◦ There is no true freedom without limits.

    ◦ A Spending Plan sets safe limits financially.

SESSION 2

Earning and Giving

The Benefits of a Spending Plan

❏ Allows us to face reality.

❏ Avoids waste.

❏ Keeps our values and priorities in the forefront.

❏ Leads to financial freedom.

⚙ Individual Activity: Benefits of a Spending Plan

Take a moment and put a checkmark by the benefit listed above that you think would most impact you.

If you're with a group, share which benefit you checked and why you checked it with one or two other people.

1. In light of what we have covered so far, review the goals you recorded on your pre-work form to see if you want to keep them the same or make any changes. If you were not able to complete this portion of the pre-work, do so now.

2. Prioritize your goals, and list the top three in the space provided:

Goal 1: _____

_____

Goal 2: _____

_____

Goal 3: _____

_____

Record Keeping

- It's simpler than it seems.

- It takes less time than you think.

- It does not require an advanced degree in mathematics.

- Tracking your expenses is not the same as budgeting!

Month *January*

Spending Record Example

Daily Variable Expenses

	Transportation		Household						Professional Services	Entertainment		
	Gas, etc.	Maint/Repair	Groceries	Clothes	Gifts	Household Items	Personal	Other		Going Out	Travel	Other
(1) Spending Plan	200	40	480	150	80	75	50	---	---	100	70	40
	64	21	186	89	17	14	16	25		22	70	22 (sitter)
	42		22	46	55	22	18			46		
	38		20	50		9				19		
	58		172			31						
			18									
			8									
			20									
(2) Total	202	21	446	185	72	76	34	25	---	87	70	22
(3) (Over)/Under	(2)	19	34	(35)	8	(1)	16	(25)	---	13	---	18
(4) Last Mo. YTD												
(5) This Mo. YTD												

- Use this page to record expenses that tend to be daily, variable expenses – often the hardest to control.
- Keep receipts throughout the day and record them at the end of the day.
- Total each category at the end of the month (line 2) and compare to the Spending Plan (line 1). Subtracting line 2 from line 1 gives you an (over) or under the budget figure for that month (line 3).
- To verify that you have made each day's entry, cross out the number at the bottom of the page that corresponds to that day's date.
- Optional: If you wish to monitor your progress as you go through the year, you can keep cumulative totals in lines 4 and 5.

~~1~~ ~~2~~ ~~3~~ ~~4~~ ~~5~~ ~~6~~ ~~7~~ ~~8~~ ~~9~~ ~~10~~ ~~11~~ ~~12~~ ~~13~~ ~~14~~ ~~15~~ ~~16~~ ~~17~~ ~~18~~ ~~19~~ ~~20~~ ~~21~~ ~~22~~ ~~23~~ ~~24~~ ~~25~~ ~~26~~ 27 28 29 30 31

Spending Record Example

Monthly Regular Expenses (generally paid by check once a month)

| | Giving | | Savings | Debt | | | Housing | | | | Auto Pmts. | Insurance | | Misc. |
	Church	Other		Credit Cards	Education	Other	Mort/Rent	Maint.	Utilities	Other		Auto/Home	Life/Med.	Cash Exp.
(1) Spending Plan	280	30	155	75	50	---	970	30	180	25	350	90	40	65
	140	20	155	75	50	---	970	---	95 (elec)	44	350		40	65
	140	10	200						31 (gas)					
									79 (tel)					
(2) Total	280	30	355	75	50	---	970	---	205	44	350	---	40	65
(3) (Over)/Under	---	---	(200)	---	---	---	---	30	(25)	(19)	---	90	---	---
(4) Last Mo. YTD														
(5) This Mo. YTD														

- This page allows you to record major monthly expenses for which you typically write just one or two checks per month.
- Entries can be recorded as the checks are written (preferably) or by referring back to the check ledger at a convenient time.
- Total each category at the end of the month (line 2) and compare to the Spending Plan (line 1). Subtracting line 2 from line 1 gives you an (over) or under the budget figure for that month (line 3).
- Use the "Monthly Assessment" section to reflect on the future actions that will be helpful in staying on course.

Monthly Assessment

Area	(Over)/Under	Reason	Future Action
Clothes	(35)	After-Christmas sales	No new clothes next month
Savings	(200)	Gift from Aunt Mary	N/A
Utilities	(25)	Electricity and phone	check phone plan
Insurance	90	Quarterly bill next month	N/A

Areas of Victory _Feels great to be ahead on savings. Thanks, Aunt Mary!_
I'm really proud of how we're doing!

Areas to Watch _Need to look hard at ways to save on electricity and phone bills._

Earning and Giving

Hints for Making Record Keeping Easier

- Keep your Spending Record form where you will see and record on it daily.

- Round off to the nearest dollar.

- Combine or rename categories.

- Have a miscellaneous cash category for small expenditures.

- Remember to assign sales tax proportionally to the appropriate categories.

Individual Activity: Spending Record Practice

Assume it's the end of the day and you've made some purchases. Using the receipts shown on the next page, fill out the Spending Record form on page 30.

Sample Receipts

MASON'S PAINT

10/14/2008   126870

Qty	Descrp	Price	Amt
1	Quart BM Int Flat	$17.49	$17.49
	Color #124		SALE

Qty	Descrp	Price	Amt
1	Quart BM Int Flat	$17.49	$17.49
	Color #643		SALE

Subtotal		$34.98
Tax 8.75%		$3.06
Total		$38.04

Neighborhood Foods
Libertyville

TUE 10142008 0306PM

Skim Fat Free Milk	$ 11.07
3 @ $3.69	
Cola 2 Liter	$ 1.39
Whole-Wheat Bread	$ 2.49
Frozen Pizza	$ 9.98
2 @ $4.99	
Large Eggs	$ 1.99
Corn Flakes	$ 2.99
Deli - Macaroni Salad	$ 3.53
Bananas - 3.05 lb	$ 1.65
Mild Salsa	$ 6.28
2 @ $3.14	
Choc Chip Ice Cream	$ 4.69
Regular Chips	$ 3.99
Flour Tortillas	$ 1.49
Salad Mix	$ 5.98
2 @ $2.99	
Sour Cream	$ 2.49
Hamburger Buns	$ 1.99
Ground Beef - 1.05 lb	$ 3.59
Low-Fat Yogurt	$ 5.52
8 @ $0.69	
Wild Rice	$ 3.99
Subtotal	$ 75.10
Tax 1	$ 1.69
Total	$ 76.79

ABC Department Store

DEPT 196 CL8

KNIT JACKET	98.00
PLU DISC 30%	29.40-
NET ITEM PRICE	68.60

DEPT 209 LS 2

KING LINEN	58.00
PLU DISC 30%	17.40-
NET ITEM PRICE	40.60
SUBTOTAL	109.20
TX 8.75%	9.56
TOTAL	118.76
10142008	11:27 AM

$1 soft drink from a machine

CHARLOTTE'S CAFÉ
BARRINGTON, ILLINOIS

TUE   10/14/08

1	CHEF'S SALAD	$8.99
	LG RASP. ICED TEA	$2.49
	CHOC LAYER CAKE	$3.49
2	ITAL. BEEF SAND	$9.99
	LG LEMONADE	$2.49
	SUBTOTAL	$27.45
	TAX 8.75%	$2.40
	TIP	$6.00
	TOTAL	$35.85

MAIN STREET GAS

DLR#9485588
GURNEE, IL

10/14/08
AUTH#72109
PUMP #2

SPECIAL	12.079G
PRICE/GAL	$4.299
FUEL TOTAL	$51.93

Month _____

Spending Record

Daily Variable Expenses

	Transportation		Household						Professional Services	Entertainment		
	Gas, etc.	Maint/Repair	Groceries	Clothes	Gifts	Household Items	Personal	Other		Going Out	Travel	Other
(1) Spending Plan												
	51.⁹³		76.⁷⁹	118.⁷⁶				38.⁰⁴		35.⁸⁵		1
(2) Total												
(3) (Over)/Under												
(4) Last Mo. YTD												
(5) This Mo. YTD												

1 | 2 | 3 | 4 | 5 | 6 | 7 | 8 | 9 | 10 | 11 | 12 | 13 | 14 | 15 | 16 | 17 | 18 | 19 | 20 | 21 | 22 | 23 | 24 | 25 | 26 | 27 | 28 | 29 | 30 | 31

- Use this page to record expenses that tend to be daily, variable expenses – often the hardest to control.
- Keep receipts throughout the day and record them at the end of the day.
- Total each category at the end of the month (line 2) and compare to the Spending Plan (line 1). Subtracting line 2 from line 1 gives you an (over) or under the budget figure for that month (line 3).
- To verify that you have made each day's entry, cross out the number at the bottom of the page that corresponds to that day's date.
- Optional: If you wish to monitor your progress as you go through the year, you can keep cumulative totals in lines 4 and 5.

⚙ Individual Activity: Which Kind of Form Will You Use?

1. Take a minute to decide if you're going to use the written form or electronic form for your record keeping over the next month, and write your decision below.

    I will use the _____ form.

2. If you are using the written form, decide where you will keep it so that it's handy, and record your decision below.

    I will keep the written form _____
    so I will see it daily.

Earning

The Pull of the Culture vs. the Mind and Heart of God

Foolish

Faithful

The Pull of the Culture

The Mind and Heart of God

Cultural Messages

• Your value is measured by your position, your paycheck, the kind of car you drive, or the house you live in.

• A little more money will solve all your problems.

The Mind and Heart of God

• Our value is not measured by what we earn or do, but by who we are: beloved sons and daughters of God.

• Work is a blessing.

• We are called to join God in the ongoing management of His creation.

The Diligent Earner

Diligent Earner: One who works with commitment, purpose, and a grateful attitude.

Work willingly at whatever you do...
Colossians 3:23 (NLT)

- Be purposeful.

    ...[Work] as though you were working for the Lord rather than for people.
    Colossians 3:23 (NLT)

    ○ We work to serve God.

    ○ We work to provide for ourselves and those dependent on us.

        ...those who won't care for their relatives ... have denied the true faith...
        1 Timothy 5:8 (NLT)

- Be grateful.

    You may say to yourself, "My power and the strength of my hands have produced this wealth for me." But remember the LORD your God, for it is he who gives you the ability to produce wealth...
    Deuteronomy 8:17-18

Practical Tips on Earning

Net Take-Home Pay

> **Net Take-Home Pay:** The amount of the paycheck after all taxes and deductions.

- Be aware of your deductions!

    ○ An online calculator to help you determine the appropriate amount to be withheld is available at www.irs.gov (search for "withholding calculator").

    ○ Choose the most cost-effective healthcare plan available to you, and don't forget to use your flex spending account if you have one.

    ○ Take advantage of any matching contributions to your 401(k) from your employer.

Variable Income

- To estimate variable income, take a *conservative* estimate of your after-tax annual income (based on your income from the past few years) and divide by twelve.

    ○ Example: $36,000 ÷ 12 = $3,000 per month

        For more information about planning with variable incomes, see p. 101 in the Appendix.

- Don't forget to put money aside for quarterly taxes.

Two Incomes

- With the first income, cover all the basics — all ongoing necessary expenses:

    - Giving

    - Saving

    - Food

    - Clothing

    - Housing

    - Transportation

- After appropriate giving and saving, the second income should be used only for "extras":

    - Accelerated debt repayment

    - Above and beyond giving

    - Special travel and entertainment

    - Additional savings

    - Other nonessentials

- All these "extras" should be paid with money saved in advance.

- If your present situation makes it impossible to meet basic expenses with one income, then put a significant amount of the second income into savings so there is money in reserve in case the second income is lost.

Raises

- What happens to your raises?

  To see how extra income from raises adds up quickly, see p. 102 in the Appendix.

- Decide ahead of time how you'll use raises, or any unexpected income, to reach your financial goals.

Key Question: How will you use any new income to reach your financial goals?

⚙ Individual Activity: Allocating New Income and Spending Plan Application

1. What will you do with your next raise or any other unexpected income? Below, record how you will allocate that income and apply it to your goals.

   Any raises or unexpected income will be allocated towards:

2. When you've finished, fill in your net income in the Income category on your Spending Plan worksheet. Since in all likelihood your income hasn't changed since you did your pre-work, you can probably copy it from your What I Spend pre-work form.

Giving

▶ ▶ ▶ Video: *The Offering*

The Pull of the Culture vs. the Mind and Heart of God

Foolish   **Faithful**

The Pull of   The Mind and
the Culture   Heart of God

Cultural Messages

- Give if it benefits you.

- Give if there is anything left over.

- Give out of a sense of duty.

The Mind and Heart of God

- There is a unique joy in giving.

> **Generous Giver:** One who gives with an obedient will, a joyful attitude, and a compassionate heart.

- We are created to give – to be channels, not reservoirs.

- Why God wants us to give:

  - As a response to God's goodness.

    Whatever is good and perfect comes down to us from God our Father…
    James 1:17 (NLT)

  - To focus on Him as our ultimate source of security.

    Don't store up treasures here on earth, where moths eat them and rust destroys them, and where thieves break in and steal. Store your treasures in heaven…
    Matthew 6:19-20a (NLT)

    "Would you be more upset to find out there was no God, or that you had no money in any of your accounts?" – Andy Stanley

  - To help achieve economic justice.

  - To bless others and to be blessed.

  - To break the hold money can have on us.

Individual Activity: The Generous Giver

After thinking through the Mind and Heart of God on giving, in what way is God nudging you? Is there an action step He wants you to take? If so, write it in the space provided below.

Action step:

SESSION 3

Giving and Saving

Practical Tips on Giving

- The biblical benchmark for giving is the tithe.

- The tithe has three characteristics:

  - It is a priority – the first thing we do with our resources.

  - It has a purpose – to further the work of God in the world.

  - It is a proportion – 10% of all we receive.

- To work toward the tithe:

  - Begin by giving something.

  > **Key Question:** How much of God's money do I need to live on?

  - Develop a long-term plan to reach the tithe.

⚙ Individual Activity: Spending Plan Application

Keeping in mind the action step you wrote for giving, consider your current financial situation and what you are becoming as a giver. Then, set a short-term goal for giving, and fill in the giving line on your Spending Plan worksheet.

The Final Act of Giving

- On average, 80-90% of net worth is in non-liquid assets such as insurance, real estate, retirement funds, etc.

For information on the giving of assets upon death, see p. 103 in the Appendix.

Saving

The Pull of the Culture vs. the Mind and Heart of God

Foolish

Faithful

The Pull of
the Culture

The Mind and
Heart of God

Cultural Messages

- If you have it, spend it, and if you don't have it, spend it anyway.

- It is futile to save.

The Mind and Heart of God

Wise Saver: One who builds, preserves, and invests with discernment.

- It is wise to save.

   The wise store up choice food and oil, but fools gulp theirs down.
   Proverbs 21:20 (TNIV)

- It is foolish, even sinful, to hoard (Luke 12:16-21).

   ○ What's the difference between saving and hoarding?

      - Saving is putting money aside for appropriate goals.

      - Hoarding is stockpiling beyond our needs or using our goals as
        excuses to build "bigger barns."

○ How can we avoid the "bigger barns" syndrome?

- Understand our tendencies.
  For more insight on your own tendencies toward money, work through the Money Autobiography located on p. P17 in the pre-work.

- Answer the question, "When is enough, enough?"

  Those who love money will never have enough…
  Ecclesiastes 5:10 (NLT)

❈ ❈ ❈ Activity: Your Money Tendency

1. Check the box below that applies to you. If you completed the Money Motivation Quiz in the pre-work, you can use those results instead.

   Money is important to me because it gives me:

   ❑ Freedom – to do what I want to do. Independence is important to me. Money means having the freedom to do what I want.

   ❑ Security – to feel safe. Stability is important to me. Money means having protection from life's uncertainties.

   ❑ Power – to get ahead in life. Success is important to me. Money means having control over the things I value most.

   ❑ Love – to buy things for others. Relationships are important to me. Money means having the means to express my love to others and to build relationships.

2. If you're in a group, team up with two or three other people and answer the following questions, or write your answers in the space provided if you're working on your own:

   - What is one way your money tendency impacts you?

- What is one step you can take to begin limiting that impact?

The Definition of Saving

- Saving is money you keep!

- Saving is not money we have lost or given up the use of – it's future spending.

The Benefit of Saving

- One huge benefit of saving is that it allows the very powerful force of compounding to work in our favor.

- Compound interest is interest earning interest, earning interest.

  ◦ Compound interest example:

    - $100 at 10% = $10 interest

    - $110 at 10% = $11 interest

    - The extra $1 is compound interest.

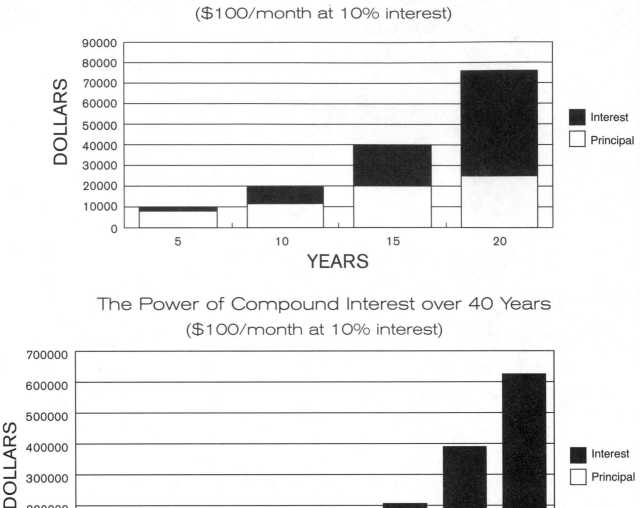

The Power of Compound Interest over 20 Years
($100/month at 10% interest)

The Power of Compound Interest over 40 Years
($100/month at 10% interest)

- The fruit of the Spirit required here is patience!

  See p. 105 in the Appendix for more information on the cumulative effect of little things over time.

- Be aware of the opportunity cost of money.

  ○ We can spend money on anything, but we can only spend it once.

Three Categories of Savings

Emergency Savings

- Prepare you for the unexpected.

- Should be at least three months of basic living expenses (such as housing, food, and transportation costs).

- Should be kept in accounts you have easy access to (like a money market fund).

Replacement Savings

- Replacement savings are for large, expected purchases.

- These savings could be invested in short-term certificates of deposit.

  - See www.bankrate.com for funds with the highest return rates.

- Use replacement savings when you can anticipate that an item will eventually need to be replaced.

  See p. 107 in the Appendix for the average life expectancy and replacement cost for various household items.

  - If you haven't built up the replacement fund before an item breaks, use emergency savings, but only if replacing the item is truly an emergency.

- Have emergency and replacement funds direct-deposited into savings.

Long-Term Savings

- Long-term savings are for planned circumstances that have long timeframes.

- Take advantage of your employer's retirement plan if available, especially if they provide matching funds.

- Don't borrow from retirement accounts!

    For more information on why it's unwise to borrow from retirement accounts, see p. 108 in the Appendix.

⚙ Individual Activity: Spending Plan Application

1. Calculate an appropriate level of emergency savings. Consider a minimum of three months of basic living expenses such as housing, food, and transportation.

2. Consider your current financial situation. Set a short-term goal for savings that will help you begin to build your emergency savings fund. If you already have an emergency savings fund, consider goals for replacement or long-term savings.

3. Fill in the savings category on your Spending Plan worksheet.

Prioritizing the Four Uses of Money

Key Question: If giving is so right and saving is so wise, why are they so hard to do?

I do not understand what I do. For what I want to do I do not do, but what I hate I do.
Romans 7:15

Cultural Order

1. Lifestyle (spending)

2. Debt

3. Saving and/or Giving

God-Honoring Order

1. Giving

2. Saving

3. Lifestyle

Transitional Phase

- Give … something

- Save … something

- Debt … maximum repayment

- Lifestyle … Spartan

  ○ Minimize spending to maximize funds available for debt repayment and emergency savings.

  ○ Example:

    - $100/month for entertainment becomes $15/month

    - $120/month for clothing becomes $25/month

    - That combined $180 a month goes towards debt repayment and emergency savings.

SESSION 4

Debt

Debt

The Pull of the Culture vs. the Mind and Heart of God

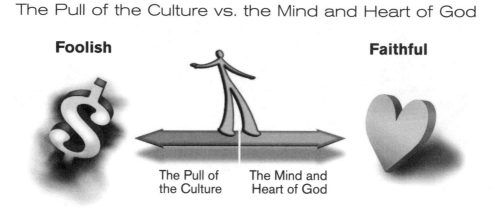

Foolish   **Faithful**

The Pull of
the Culture

The Mind and
Heart of God

- "OK" debt has two characteristics:

  1. It is incurred on something that has the strong potential to increase in value (not a depreciating or consumptive item).

  2. It can be repaid under *today's* circumstances – not hoped-for circumstances in the future.

- One cultural myth is that debt is expected and unavoidable.

▶ ▶ ▶ Video: *The Debtor on the Street*

The Cautious Debtor

Cautious Debtor: One who avoids entering into debt, is careful and strategic when incurring debt, and always repays debt.

Economic Danger of Debt

- Compound interest works against you.

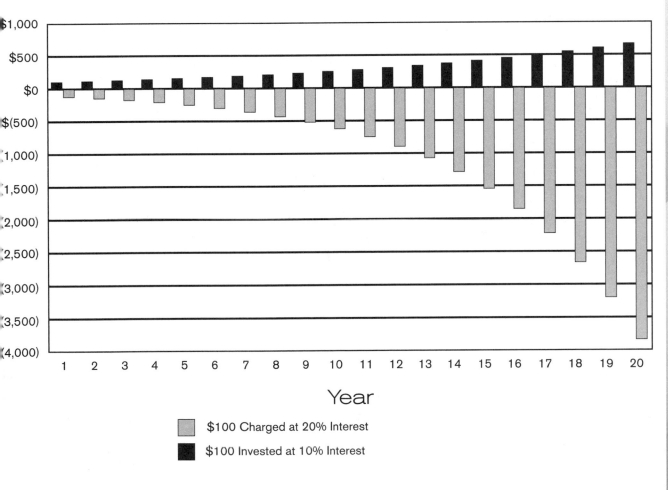

The Power of Compound Interest

$100 Charged at 20% Interest

$100 Invested at 10% Interest

Biblical Guidelines

- Repay debt.

  The wicked borrow and do not repay...
  Psalm 37:21

- Avoid debt.

  ...the borrower is servant to the lender.
  Proverbs 22:7

Three Spiritual Dangers of Debt

1. Presumes on the future.

   Why, you do not even know what will happen tomorrow...
   James 4:14

2. Denies God the opportunity to show His love and provision and to teach us through denial.

   These things dominate the thoughts of unbelievers all over the world, but your Father already knows your needs. Seek the Kingdom of God above all else, and he will give you everything you need.
   Luke 12:30-31 (NLT)

3. Fosters envy and greed.

   ...Beware! Guard against every kind of greed. Life is not measured by how much you own.
   Luke 12:15 (NLT)

Five Kinds of Debt

1. Home mortgage

2. Auto

3. Education

4. Business

5. Consumer

Credit Cards

- Use credit cards wisely.

- Studies have shown that credit card users tend to spend more.

  o Using a credit card is psychologically different than using cash.

  o Unless we download or monitor transactions regularly, we have no awareness of how much we've charged until the next statement arrives.

- Credit card rules:

  1. Use only for budgeted items.

  2. Pay the balance in full every month.

  3. If you violate rule one or rule two, cut up your cards.

- Credit card tips:

  ○ Have only one card (maybe a second as a backup).

  ○ Consider the wise use of a debit card.

    • Be careful not to overdraw your account, which incurs fees.

  ○ Deduct the amount from your checkbook or electronic register as you go.

  ○ Make sure that online purchases are in your Spending Plan.

Individual Activity: Credit Cards

In the space below, write down one action step you want to take regarding your credit card(s).

Action Step:

Paying Down Debt

Credit Card Debt and Repayment Example

You owe $7,200 @ 18%		
Minimum Payment = 3% of the balance or $10 — whichever is greater		
You Pay	Total Paid	Time
$ Minimum/month	$14,277	20 yrs. 11 mos.
$216/month	$10,150	47 mos.
$216+100/month	$8,848	28 mos.

Key Question: Are you committed enough to freeing yourself from the bondage of debt to find a little over three dollars a day somewhere in your expenditures that could go to debt repayment?

Process for Accelerating Debt Repayment

1. Incur no new debt!

2. List all your debts in order from smallest to largest.

3. Pay off your smallest debt first.

4. As a debt is repaid, roll the amount you were paying to the next largest debt.

5. Continue that strategy until all debts are paid.

   For more guidance on creating a debt repayment plan, see p. 109 in the Appendix.

Debt

Sample Debt Reduction Plan

Item	Amount Owed	Interest	Minimum Monthly Payment	Additional Payment $150	Payment Plan and Pay-off Dates				
					3 Months	6 Months	15 Months	22 Months	26 Months
Sears	$372	18.0	$15	$165	paid!				
Doctor	$550	0	$20	$20	$185	paid!			
Visa	$1980	19.0	$40	$40	$40	$225	paid!		
MasterCard	$2369	16.9	$50	$50	$50	$50	$275	paid!	
Auto	$7200	6.9	$259	$259	$259	$259	$259	$534	paid!
Total	$12,471		$384	$534	$534	$534	$534	$534	0

- The first and second columns list to whom the debt is owed and the amount owed. Debts are listed in the order of lowest to highest amount.
- The third and fourth columns list the interest rate and the minimum monthly payment for each debt.
- The fifth column indicates the amount of additional payment above the minimum that can be made and adds that amount to the minimum payment for the first (smallest) debt listed.
- The remaining columns show how, as each debt is paid, the payment for it is rolled down to the next debt. Pay-off dates can be calculated in advance or simply recorded as they are achieved.

To access an electronic version of this form for your own use, go to www.willowcreek.com/freedup

Individual Activity: Spending Plan Application

1. Using your pre-work information from the What I Own and What I Owe form, list each of your debts and fill in the monthly minimum payments on your Spending Plan worksheet. (If you did not complete the pre-work, estimate your monthly minimum payment for each debt.)

2. Set a tentative goal for how much additional payment you plan to make each month.

3. Apply this additional payment to your smallest debt.

Debt Repayment Is a Great Investment!

- Immediate

- Tax Free

- Guaranteed

- High rate of return

Debt Is Often the Symptom, Not the Problem

- Discover and eliminate the root of the issue.

- Limit your exposure to temptation.

- Give up on one-upping your neighbors.

▶ ▶ ▶ Video: *Out of Debt*

⚙ Individual Activity: Reaction to *Out of Debt*

1. Look at the amount of money now going to debt repayment and imagine the freedom you will feel when you are out from under that burden, and the financial goals you can achieve with those resources. If you want to, use the space below to write down your thoughts and reflections.

    My thoughts:

2. When you're done, take a moment to talk with God about the steps you want to take regarding your debt. If you're with a group, you may want to pray together.

SESSION 5

Spending

Spending

The Pull of the Culture vs. the Mind and Heart of God

Foolish

Faithful

The Pull of the Culture

The Mind and Heart of God

Cultural Messages

- Things bring happiness.

- Possessions define who we are.

- The more we have, the more we should spend.

- Spending is a competition.

The Mind and Heart of God

Prudent Spender: One who enjoys the fruits of their labor yet guards against materialism.

Three Biblical Financial Principles

1. Beware of idols.

   You shall have no other gods before me. You shall not make for yourself an idol in the form of anything in heaven above or on the earth beneath or in the waters below. … I, the LORD your God, am a jealous God…
   Deuteronomy 5:7-9

   They exchanged the truth of God for a lie, and worshiped and served created things rather than the Creator…
   Romans 1:25

2. Guard against greed.

   …Beware! Guard against every kind of greed. Life is not measured by how much you own.
   Luke 12:15 (NLT)

   Give us each day our daily bread.
   Luke 11:3

   …give me neither poverty nor riches! Give me just enough to satisfy my needs.
   Proverbs 30:8 (NLT)

3. Be content.

   I know what it is to be in need, and I know what it is to have plenty. I have learned the secret of being content in any and every situation, whether well fed or hungry, whether living in plenty or in want.
   Philippians 4:12

   ○ Contentment with and gratitude for what we have is the antidote to greed and envy.

      Command those who are rich in this present world not to be arrogant nor to put their hope in wealth, which is so uncertain, but to put their hope in God, who richly provides us with everything for our enjoyment. Command them to do good, to be rich in good deeds, and to be generous and willing to share.
      1 Timothy 6:17-18

   ○ When we practice moderation and learn contentment, we become free to be generous and a blessing to others.

Driving Your Stake

Key Question: Are you willing to "drive your stake" lifestyle-wise?

- Driving your stake means you are willing to declare, "Enough is enough."

- When you drive your stake, you distinguish between your true needs and your wants (what the culture says you need).

Individual Activity: Driving Your Stake Lifestyle-Wise

Use the space below to answer the following question: What would it mean for me to drive my stake lifestyle-wise?

My thoughts:

Housing

Mortgage/Taxes/Rent

- Consider the issue of renting versus owning.

- Consider prepayment of your mortgage.

    To see how extra payments can significantly reduce your mortgage, see p. 112 of the Appendix.

- Beware of basing a mortgage on two incomes.

    For more information on the financial advantages of buying a smaller home, see p. 124 in the Appendix.

- Exercise extreme caution with regard to equity loans.

- Consider renting out an empty bedroom.

Maintenance and Repairs

- Become a Mr. or a Ms. "Fix-it" or find a friend with whom you can barter services.

Utilities

- Control the thermostat.

- Use phones wisely.

- Evaluate options for Internet and cable services.

    For more tips on saving on utility expenses, see p. 123 of the Appendix.

⚙ Individual Activity: Spending Plan Application

1. Look at your pre-work form for what you currently spend for housing. If you didn't complete the pre-work, use your best estimate of housing expenses. The percentage guidelines on the Spending Plan worksheet can help you.

2. Consider some of the issues discussed regarding housing. Write down at least one action step that you plan to take under this category.

Action Step:

3. Set short-term goals for housing expenses, and fill in this category of your Spending Plan worksheet.

Auto/Transportation

- The least expensive car you can drive is the one you already own.

- It is not economically wise to buy a new, never-owned car.

- There are no economic advantages to leasing.

- The time to get rid of an old car is when it costs more to maintain the car than what the car is actually worth.

  - The average reliable life of a new car is 13 years and 145,000 miles, but the average trade-in occurs at 4.5 years and 55,000 miles.

Pay Cash for Your Next Car

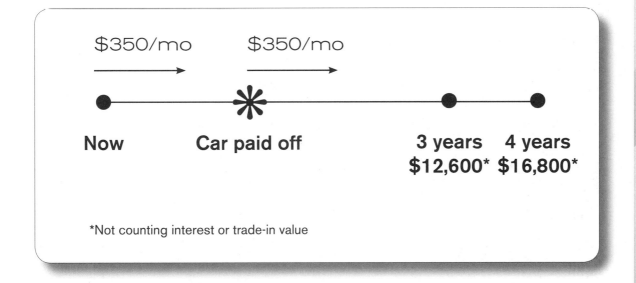

$350/mo $350/mo

Now   Car paid off   3 years   4 years
                                    $12,600* $16,800*

*Not counting interest or trade-in value

Insurance

Auto Insurance

- Choose the highest deductible you can afford.

  - "Catastrophic" is the key word for insurance.

- Shop around.

  - Use Web sites and rating services like A.M. Best Company (www.ambest.com) to evaluate insurance providers.

- Combine policies (home and car) for a discount.

- Look for other discounts.

- Consider dropping collision coverage on an older car.

Life Insurance

- Consider renewable term insurance.

- Consider whether life insurance is necessary.

- Find a trusted professional to help you review your options.

Other

- Consider disability insurance.

- Consider long-term care insurance when you reach your fifties.

Individual Activity: Spending Plan Application

1. Look at your pre-work form for what you currently spend on the auto/ transportation and insurance categories. If you didn't complete the pre-work, use your best estimate of expenses. The percentage guidelines on the Spending Plan worksheet can help you.

2. Consider any ways you can reduce these expenses. Write down at least one action step you plan to take.

Action Step:

3. Set goals for these categories, and fill in your Spending Plan worksheet.

Household/Personal, Entertainment, and Professional Services

⚙ Individual Activity: Spending Plan Application

1. Fill in the Miscellaneous Small Cash Expenditures category if you have not already.

2. Look at your pre-work for what you currently spend on Household/Personal, Entertainment, and Professional Services. If you didn't complete the pre-work, use your best estimates of expenses. The percentage guidelines on the Spending Plan worksheet can help you.

3. Next, select three or four categories you think have the most potential to be reduced, and read the information on pages 72–84 pertaining to these expenses. Write down at least one idea that can help you reduce expenses in each of those categories, and write a short-term goal for each on your Spending Plan worksheet.

   Ideas:

4. Set goals for all remaining categories and enter them on your Spending Plan worksheet.

5. Review your entire worksheet and if there are categories that you have not already completed, do so now.

6. Total all your expenses and **fill out the box in the lower right corner of your Spending Plan worksheet**. At this time, don't be concerned about whether or not the income and expenses balance.

Household/Personal

Entertainment

Professional Services

Groceries

Monthly Food Costs*				
Family Size	Thrifty	Low Cost	Moderate	Liberal
2	$377	$418	$515	$634
4	$525	$673	$832	$1,022

* Source: USDA Center for Nutrition, U.S. average, December 2007

Groceries can be a budget buster. Proof that significant savings can occur in the food budget is reflected in the government statistics above showing the amount spent for food on a monthly basis by families that are thrifty versus those that are liberal in their spending. Almost twice as much is spent on food by the liberal shoppers. This is a key area of the budget at which to look very carefully.

Here are a number of tips for reducing your grocery bill:

- Make a list – and stick to it (perhaps the single most effective way to control food costs).
- Use coupons.
- Buy private label brands.
- Buy bulk, especially when non-perishables you regularly use are on sale.
- Shop at discounted food stores.
- Beware of marketing techniques that encourage impulse purchases.
- Make up a price list on common items so you can recognize a good deal.
- Remember that convenience foods cost more.
- Buy fruits and vegetables in season and check out local farmers markets if available.
- Plant a vegetable garden.
- Eliminate snack foods.
- Don't go overboard on organics.
- Planning meals for a week or more in advance (particularly in conjunction with advertised sales) and freezing for future use saves money and time on both purchase and preparation.
- Saving money on food does not mean sacrificing nutritional value. In fact, many of the items which are comparatively most expensive (snack foods, sugared cereals, soft drinks, etc.) have the least nutritional value. You can eat inexpensively and healthfully.

Clothes/Dry Cleaning

Clothing can be a very emotional area. Sometimes we buy clothes we don't need just to feel better about ourselves or we pay exorbitant prices because we feel our self worth is based on what we wear. If you sense that's true about you, we encourage you to seek help in getting to the bottom of those feelings. God doesn't want you pegging your self worth on what you wear.

If you are a parent, beware of reinforcing the cultural message to your child that their value is based on what they wear by buying them clothes with all the right labels (and potentially busting the budget in the process).

Here's some startling statistics:
- Ten percent of clothing gets worn 90 percent of the time.
- One-third of clothing never gets worn.

These statistics may be because we bring new clothes home and they don't look the same under our lighting as they did in the store, they don't match an outfit the way we thought they would, they don't fit quite right, or we just didn't need them in the first place.

It's amazing how few clothes one could really get by on. If you had three pairs of pants, three shirts, and three pieces of outerwear like jackets or sweaters, and if they mixed and matched, you could have twenty-seven different outfits. And how many pairs of shoes do we really need?

The point is, buy sensibly. Buy classic styles that won't quickly go out of fashion and look for ways to mix and match color schemes. An interesting exercise might be to tag clothing at the beginning of the season and see which still have the tag at the end of the season (ie. have not been worn) and then give those away.

Here are some additional tips on clothing:

- Challenge yourself to make it through a season change without buying new clothes unless absolutely necessary.
- Buy during the off-season.
- Shop at discount stores and consignment shops.
- Welcome hand-me-downs.
- Buy non-name brand clothing.*
- Trade outgrown children's clothes with other families.
- Shop rummage and garage sales for children's clothing.
- Buy fabrics that don't require expensive dry cleaning.

* Interesting note: In a February 2000 *National Geographic* article, the author reported on his visit to a clothing plant in the Chinese city of Birobdzhau in which a "woman was sewing labels into identical blouses. Both labels listed the recommended U.S. retail price. One said, 'Old Navy $18'; the other, 'Chaps Ralph Lauren $38'. The manufacturing costs for each were identical: $5 for labor and $2.50 for material …"

Gifts

Perhaps you were surprised by how much gifts add up when you did your gift list in the pre-work. Gifts can be a significant item in the budget. And the ironic thing is that we often are creating financial stress for ourselves to buy gifts for folks who already have everything they need and a lot more besides. The key principle is that the cost of the gift is not a reflection of your love. Remember that not only are the best things in life free, the best things in life aren't things.

There are lots of ideas for reducing your gift expenditures:

- Make a gift list.
- Have a gift budget.
- Make or bake gifts.
- Invite people for a special meal.
- Write a letter of appreciation to the person (what you really appreciate about them and your relationship to them) rather than buying a gift.
- Give to a charity in a person's name. The money goes where it's really needed, and the person knows they've been thought of (and you may even get a tax break).
- Give coupons for doing things for someone like chores, backrubs, etc.
- Shop at low-cost stores. Dollar stores are good choices for inexpensive children's gifts.
- Make agreements between families to limit the amount spent, the number of persons to whom gifts are given, etc. Draw names from a hat to determine whom you'll give to.
- Be on the lookout for appropriate gifts year-round so you can get them when on sale.
- Save on the cost of greeting cards:
    - Buy next year's cards right after this year's holiday.
    - Buy cards at dollar stores.
    - Make your own.

Books/Magazines/Music

Two important questions regarding this category:

1. Do you actually read or listen to it? The cheapest subscription or sale price in the world is still not a bargain if we never get around to reading or listening to the material.

2. The second question may be more important than the first. *Should you read or listen to the material?* The saying, "Garbage in, garbage out" applies to the human mind as well as computers. Take to heart these words:

> *…whatever is true, whatever is honorable, whatever is right, whatever is pure, whatever is lovely, whatever is of good repute, if there is any excellence and if anything worthy of praise, dwell on these things.*
> Philippians 4:8 (NASB)

The following ideas may help you save money in this category:

• Use the library – get a return on your taxes. (Libraries sometimes have free tickets to local concerts and cultural events as well.)

• Share subscriptions with a friend or neighbor.

• Buy paperbacks instead of hardcover books.

• Utilize free Web sites to gain access to material that appears in periodicals and newspapers.

• Buy used books online.

Allowances

Age four or five is not too young for children to learn the basic biblical principles for handling their money, but for children to learn to handle money wisely, they must have some with which to work. Allowances can be the means by which they receive money and can be an excellent teaching tool.

Here's a technique one father used with his small children. Once a month he sat them down, and they would talk about their allowance. He would give each of them their allowance of one dollar in 10 dimes. He would also give them each a series of paper cups. On each cup, he would write what the cups represented. He'd take the money and count it out while the kids got all excited. Then, he'd ask them, "Did you do your chores this month? Did you honor Mom and Dad?" Then, he told them he was going to give them their allowance. He'd say, "Here's the first dime. Where does it go? Put it right in the cup marked "Gifts for Jesus." Where does the second dime go? Savings. You should always save something of what you receive. Where does the third dime go? Take the dime and put it in the food cup. Your food right now can be bubble gum or candy. Where's the fourth dime go? Housing. You've got to have shelter, and shelter costs money. But as long as you're living with Mom and me, you can take the money for shelter and put it into savings." The next cup went to gifts for others like Father's Day, Mother's Day, or birthdays for brothers or sisters. The last cup was for whatever they wanted to do – for spending!

These same kids then graduated to more advanced tools like a written budget with categories for things like school lunch and gym shoes. In high school they transitioned into covering their own expenses out of their earnings and used budgeting software to keep on target.

Other families have used similar ideas and given their children three banks, one each for giving, saving, and spending. Each bank received a portion of any money the child obtained.

An excellent resource with many additional ideas is *Debt-Proof Your Kids* by Mary Hunt.

Personal Technology

With technology changing so rapidly, it is easy to get caught up in the "need" to have the latest and greatest new development. However, if you don't really need it, having the latest technology can be a costly venture. Consider the following hints to hold down costs in this area:

- Think about purchasing refurbished computers, cameras, mp3 players, etc. instead of new. Some items marked "refurbished" are actually brand new; they were simply returned by people who decided they didn't want them.

- Avoid the most expensive offerings. Often the highest-end models include features most people rarely use. Computers with a slightly slower processor come with a substantial price discount and little or no observable reduction in performance.

- Recognize that even if your technology is no longer state-of-the-art, if it still adequately performs the tasks you bought it for, you don't "need" to upgrade. Much of the marketing for technology products blurs the line between needs and wants.

- See if the organization you work for will buy the device for you if it aids you in your work.

- Take the time to research your purchase once you determine that you will benefit from that piece of technology. Look for Web sites to get third-party and owner reviews. Use price comparison Web sites to get the lowest prices.

- Take a pass on the extended warranty. According to *Consumer Reports*, extended warranties are seldom worth the cost.

Education

Precollege

For a variety of reasons, some of us struggle with the decision of private versus public school for our children. This is a very sensitive, even volatile, topic. It is mentioned here because of the financial implications of that decision.

In making the decision, recognize that the number one influence on our children's development is what takes place in the home. In light of that, I believe that a foremost goal should be to ensure that the environment of the home is protected. Thus an important question is whether sending your children to private school will put you into a debt situation.

If the answer is yes and considering the stress that debt causes on a family, it would be difficult under those circumstances to justify paying for private education. This is not an anti-private education statement; it is simply speaking to a financial reality. If you are set on private education, look in your Spending Plan and determine what other sacrifices you are willing to make to fund that education without placing financial stress upon the family.

College

If you want to help your children financially with their college education, start saving early. Allow the cumulative effect of compound interest to work for you and receive tax advantages by saving in a 529 College Savings Plan or a Coverdell Education Savings Account.

Early on, share with your children that they have a responsibility to assist with their college expenses through money they begin saving in junior high or earlier. Set the goal of having no college debt after graduation. Set the expectation of working ten to fifteen hours per week while in college. No curriculum is so difficult that a student cannot work ten to fifteen hours a week and still have time to study and socialize. That, combined with full-time vacation and summer work, can easily generate $5,000 to $10,000 a year toward expenses.

College continued

Some further ideas for reducing college costs include:

- Opt for a state university. You may think your child needs an Ivy League education in order to be successful. However, just 10 percent of CEOs at the top 500 companies graduated from such schools. Most went to state universities or to less-known private colleges.*

- By all means be diligent in exploring scholarships … but beware of offers to help you find scholarships for a fee (sometimes hundreds of dollars). Such assistance often amounts to referral of potential scholarship sources that a little effort on your part can uncover.

- Attend a two-year college and then transfer to a four-year institution. The cost of the first two years will be much lower – in addition to the potential savings of living at home those two years. The student's degree will still be from the four-year school. Be sure the four-year school they plan to attend accepts credits from the two-year school.

- Take part in a cooperative program that alternates periods of study with work experience in which the student can earn a significant portion of the next period's tuition.

- Work for a year before entering college.

- Serve in the military and use government grants to then pay for college.

- Shop for textbooks online.

- Be cautious about student loans. It has become a common assumption that student loans are a good thing – a low-interest way to finance an education. While interest rates for student loans do tend to be favorable, they are still a form of debt and must be repaid. Too often young couples enter marriage with combined student loans totaling tens of thousands of dollars – a huge financial burden with which to begin married life.

  Some college advisors and financial aid officers counsel that tuition should not figure into the decision of where to attend. Their line of reasoning is that the higher the cost, the more financial aid the student will qualify for. But the fact that often goes unmentioned is that 85 percent of student financial aid comes in the form of loans (that's a nice way of saying *debt*). The relative cost of a given college should logically be a factor in the decision of where to attend.

  Some loans may be necessary, but carefully consider alternatives that minimize loans as you plan for college expenses. It's possible (and preferable!) to complete college without a loan.

* Carol Hymowitz, "Any College Will Do," *Wall Street Journal*, September 18, 2006.

Pets

Americans spend more than $40 billion each year on their pets. That's a whole lot of cat food, dog treats, and fish tanks! Here are some ideas for saving on pet expenses:

- Just as when buying for the people in your household, use coupons and shop for pet supplies at discount stores.

- Look for pet supplies on the Internet where they are often less expensive.

- Consider making your own pet food. Recipes abound on the Internet.

- Keep your pet healthy by making sure it gets enough exercise. Long walks can reduce your veterinarian bills and may even reduce your own doctor bills.

- Instead of boarding your pet while on vacation, swap pet watching duties with friends or neighbors.

Entertainment: Going Out

Entertainment is much more enjoyable if you are not anxious about how you will pay for it. Consider the following options for spending less on this category.

- Go out to your favorite expensive restaurant, but go for dessert only. Enjoy the ambiance at a fraction of the cost.

- Order tap water with a slice of lemon rather than drinks that you pay for. The difference in your final bill can be substantial.

- Go to matinee or second-run movies, or wait for them to come out on DVD (then check if they're available free from the library).

- Pack lunches and snacks when going on family outings.

- Trade babysitting duties with another family.

- Take advantage of free or low-cost local attractions – free days at museums, park district offerings, library programs, etc.

- Entertain friends in your home. Enjoy a potluck meal together. Play board games. Rediscover how both your relationships and your bank accounts can grow from doing so.

- Walks in the park and drives in the country can provide times of good conversation, relaxation, and, in the case of walking, some good exercise.

Entertainment: Travel

With the costs of transportation, lodging, and meals on the rise, travel expenses and vacations must be carefully planned for and budgeted, or their costs lowered by seeking less expensive alternatives. An important question is if two weeks of expensive fun is worth 50 weeks (or more!) of anguish over how to pay for it.

Some tips for lowering vacation costs include:

- Take shorter trips.

- Travel in the off season.

- Stay with friends or relatives to save on hotel costs.

- Cut food costs by taking food along, traveling with a cooler in the car, and staying where breakfast is included in the cost (or at least, where children eat free).

- Take advantage of savings on the Internet – do your research.

- Try camping. It is the experience most often cited as the most cherished childhood memory. See if you can borrow and share equipment with friends. There is no need for all of us to own a tent and other equipment we use only a few times a year.

- Understand that it is not the birthright of every child to go to expensive destinations like Disney World, nor is it an essential experience for their normal growth and development. If such an experience can fit within your Spending Plan, good. If not, be assured that your child will be better served by your not suffering the effects of the resultant debt.

Entertainment: Other

The "Other" area under Entertainment contains several expenses.

A major expense (under Fitness/Sports) can be membership at a fitness center. Care of our bodies is part of biblical stewardship. The question is if you actually use the membership. Even if you do, consider if there is a less expensive way to stay in shape. Basic exercises at home, a good walking program, and wise eating may be all that's necessary.

Hobbies are quite legitimate and good for our psychological well-being. But because we tend to really enjoy our hobbies, the money spent on them can easily get out of hand. Buy used equipment for your hobbies and sports. Build hobby expenses into the Spending Plan and then stick with it. If your hobby is too expensive, find a less expensive alternative.

Professional Services

Child Care

No one would advocate anything but the very best child care. Obviously, working single parents need some form of child care. But married parents should be sure they have carefully evaluated both the financial and the relational costs of two working parents.

Financially, the spendable income from the second salary may not warrant the sacrifice made after subtracting costs such as child care, taxes, transportation, clothing, more meals out, less time to shop carefully, and a host of other smaller costs associated with both parents working. Relational costs include such things as less time together and added stress and fatigue.

An excellent book entitled *Two Incomes and Still Broke?* by Linda Kelly speaks to these issues.

Other Professional Services: Attorneys, Accountants, and Counselors

When considering your need for other professional services, be sure you are being a wise and educated client. If you feel your attorney or accountant is billing a lot of hours but not getting the job done, or if you have been seeing a counselor for an extended period of time and feel the relationship is moving you toward continued dependence rather than independence, perhaps it is time to re-evaluate the services you are receiving.

When choosing a professional service provider and whether to continue using their services:
- Use good judgment.
- Seek referrals.
- Ask good questions.
- Evaluate progress.

SESSION 6

Adjusting the Spending Plan and Commitment

Adjusting the Spending Plan

Three Possible Scenarios

1. Income equals expenses.

2. Income exceeds expenses.

3. Expenses exceed income.

How to Bring Income and Expenses into Balance

1. Increase income.

    °   Simply increasing income does not deal with the root problem of why expenses exceed income.

2. Sell assets to pay off some debt.

    °   This may be wise but also does not deal with the root problem.

3. Reduce expenses to live within your existing income.

    °   Do I have optional expenses I can eliminate?

    °   Do I have variable expenses I can further reduce?

    °   Can I eliminate any assumptions about "fixed" expenses?

Key Question: How serious are you?

A. If income equals or exceeds expenses, prayerfully and carefully review all categories to see if the margin can be increased further, and then reflect on how that margin can best be used to further your goals.

Write down at least one action step you plan to take, and make any adjustments to your Spending Plan worksheet.

Action Step:

B. If your expenses exceed your income, prayerfully and carefully review all the categories to see where you can reduce expenses.

Write down at least one action step you plan to take to adjust your Spending Plan. Then, adjust the plan and bring it into balance as best you can.

Action Step:

If you are having difficulty balancing your Spending Plan, seek assistance from a trained person at church, a trusted friend who is good with personal finances, or the local Consumer Credit Counseling Services office (1-800-388-2227, www.nfcc.org).

Revisiting Record Keeping

Benefits of Record Keeping

- Gives accurate data.

- Improves marital communication.

- Allows for midcourse corrections.

- Provides a form of accountability.

Three Systems

- Written record

- Envelope

- Electronic

Envelope System

> **Envelope System:** A tangible way to designate money for various expenses.

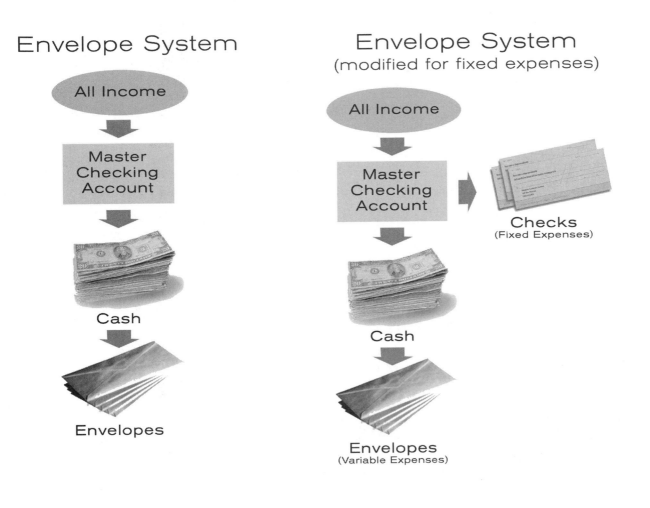

Envelope System

All Income → Master Checking Account → Cash → Envelopes

Envelope System
(modified for fixed expenses)

All Income → Master Checking Account → Cash → Envelopes (Variable Expenses)

Checks (Fixed Expenses)

Written Record System

See Spending Record example on next page.

Month _January_

Spending Record Example

Daily Variable Expenses

	Transportation		Household						Professional Services	Entertainment		
	Gas, etc.	Maint/Repair	Groceries	Clothes	Gifts	Household Items	Personal	Other		Going Out	Travel	Other
(1) Spending Plan	200	40	480	150	80	75	50	---	---	100	70	40
	64	21	186	89	17	14	16	25		22	70	22 (sitter)
	42		22	46	55	22	18			46		
	38		20	50		9				19		
	85		172			31						
			81									
			8									
			20									
(2) Total	202	21	446	185	72	76	34	25	---	87	70	22
(3) (Over)/Under	(2)	19	34	(35)	8	(1)	16	(25)	---	13	---	81
(4) Last Mo. YTD												
(5) This Mo. YTD												

X X X X X X X X X X X X X X X X X X X 20 21 22 23 24 25 26 27 28 29 30 31

- Use this page to record expenses that tend to be daily, variable expenses – often the hardest to control.
- Keep receipts throughout the day and record them at the end of the day.
- Total each category at the end of the month (line 2) and compare to the Spending Plan (line 1). Subtracting line 2 from line 1 gives you an (over) or under the budget figure for that month (line 3).
- To verify that you have made each day's entry, cross out the number at the bottom of the page that corresponds to that day's date.
- Optional: If you wish to monitor your progress as you go through the year, you can keep cumulative totals in lines 4 and 5.

Spending Record Example

Monthly Regular Expenses (generally paid by check once a month)

| | Giving | | Savings | Debt | | | Housing | | | | Auto Pmts. | Insurance | | Misc. |
	Church	Other		Credit Cards	Education	Other	Mort/Rent	Maint.	Utilities	Other		Auto/Home	Life/Med.	Cash Exp.
(1) Spending Plan	280	30	155	75	50	---	970	30	180	25	350	90	40	65
	140	20	155	75	50	---	970	---		44	350	---	40	65
	140	10	200						95 (elec)					
									31 (gas)					
									79 (tel)					
(2) Total	280	30	355	75	50	---	970	---	205	44	350	---	40	65
(3) (Over)/Under	---	---	(200)	---	---	---	---	30	(25)	(19)	---	90	---	---
(4) Last Mo. YTD														
(5) This Mo. YTD														

- This page allows you to record major monthly expenses for which you typically write just one or two checks per month.
- Entries can be recorded as the checks are written (preferably) or by referring back to the check ledger at a convenient time.
- Total each category at the end of the month (line 2) and compare to the Spending Plan (line 1). Subtracting line 2 from line 1 gives you an (over) or under the budget figure for that month (line 3).
- Use the "Monthly Assessment" section to reflect on the future actions that will be helpful in staying on course.

Monthly Assessment

Area	(Over)/Under	Reason	Future Action
Clothes	(35)	After-Christmas Sales	No new clothes next month
Savings	(200)	Gift from Aunt Mary	N/A
Utilities	(25)	Electricity and phone	check phone plan
Insurance	90	Quarterly bill next month	N/A

Areas of Victory *Feels great to be ahead on savings. Thanks, Aunt Mary!*
I'm really proud of how we're doing!

Areas to Watch *Need to look hard at ways to save on electricity and phone bills.*

Adjusting the Spending Plan

Electronic System

- You will need to invest time to learn the program and set up your accounts.

- Make sure you are using the functions that allow you to set spending targets and compare actual and planned spending.

⚙ Individual Activity: Selecting Your Record-Keeping System

1. Select which record-keeping system you plan to use to implement your Spending Plan: envelope, written record, electronic, or a combination.

   I will use the _____ system.

2. If you plan on using the written or electronic systems, transfer the numbers from your Spending Plan worksheet to the first lines of the blank Spending Record form on pages 147 and 148. You can use those numbers to help you set up your electronic record-keeping system.

   If you plan on using the envelope system, fill in each box under the Envelopes section on page 143, showing the category and dollar amounts. Under the Checks/Automatic Withdrawal section, write in any expenses you plan to pay with a check or automatic withdrawal.

Dealing with Implementation Issues

- If you receive more than one paycheck per month, create a plan for which expenses will be paid out of each paycheck.

  For a sample plan, see p. 127 in the Appendix.

- If you have money accumulating in certain categories, transfer funds from those categories into a short-term savings account.

  - Use a simple ledger to keep track of how much money in the account is in each category.

    For a sample ledger, see p. 128 in the Appendix.

⚙ Individual Activity: Obstacles

1. Write down the biggest obstacles you expect to encounter as you implement your Spending Plan and record-keeping system.

   My biggest obstacle(s):

2. If you are in a group, share what you've written with one or two other people.

Dealing with Emergencies

- Keep your commitment not to incur new debt.

- Look at your Spending Plan to see where else you may be able to save money.

- Think creatively.

- Let God's people know of your need.

Review and Commitment

The Pull of the Culture vs. the Mind and Heart of God

Foolish   **Faithful**

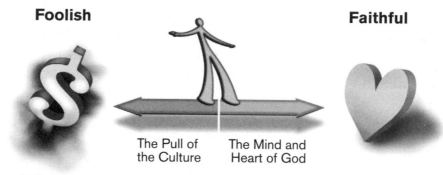

The Pull of   The Mind and
the Culture   Heart of God

- When we move faithfully toward God, we become a:

  ○ Diligent Earner

  ○ Generous Giver

  ○ Wise Saver

  ○ Cautious Debtor

  ○ Prudent Spender

- The more we become financially faithful, the closer we get to being financially free.

▶ ▶ ▶ Video: *Financial Freedom*

✳ Individual Activity: Becoming Financially Faithful, Financially Free

Write your answer to the following question in the space provided below: If you could become financially faithful and experience true financial freedom, what would your life be like?

My answer:

✦

Commitment Plan

I will begin implementing my Spending Plan and keeping records by _____.

My accountability partner will be _____.

I will pray daily for God's help and encouragement.

☩

Keeping Your Commitment

- Commit to using your Spending Plan and record-keeping system for at least ninety days.

- Do not become discouraged after the first month – adjustments are normal.

- Seek assistance, if needed.

God Is Able

- With God's help, you can do it!

Appendix Contents

> > >

Contents

Earning

Determining an Average Month for Variable Income

The key to determining a budget in the case of a variable income (due to sales commissions or being self-employed, etc.) is to make a conservative estimate of net income for the coming year. Where possible, this would be done on the basis of the past several years' income. Conservative means not allowing one really good year to unduly influence the estimate for the coming year.

For example, if the past three years' net income were $37,000, $40,000, and $54,000 (a really good year!), a *conservative* estimate for the coming year might be in the range of $44,000, not $56,000. The assumption is that this year may not be the exceptionally good year last year was.

In this example, a monthly budget would be $44,000 divided by 12 or $3,667. In the months when income exceeds $3,667, the excess would be put in a short-term savings account to be drawn on in months when income is less than $3,667.

A wise approach to variable income also includes predetermining the best use of any additional funds, in the event actual income exceeds estimated income for the year. Thoughtful consideration before the fact will prevent impulsive decisions if and when the money becomes available, avoiding regrets afterward that it had not been utilized in some other, better way.

What Happens to Your Raises?

Most of the time, the extra money we earn in raises just gets used up. A few months later, we're not quite sure where it went. Yet, even a modest raise on a modest salary can add up to a significant amount of additional income in just a few years.

A 4% Annual Raise on a $30,000 Salary

	Year 1	Year 2	Year 3
4% raise	$31,200	$32,448	$33,745
Base Salary	$30,000	$30,000	$30,000
Additional Income	$1,200	$2,448	$3,745
Total additional income in three years = $7,393			

Consider the example in the chart above: a $30,000 salary and a 4 percent raise over a three-year period.

- The first year there is a $1,200 increase (4 percent of $30,000).

- The second-year salary is then $32,448, an additional margin of $2,448 from the original salary of $30,000.

- The third-year salary increases to $33,745, producing an increase from the original $30,000 of $3,745.

The total additional income in that three-year period adds up to almost $7,400 – nearly one-fourth of the original salary! And that's just a three-year period! Taxes obviously impact the amount not given to charitable causes, but even the after-tax amount accumulates to a significant figure.

Deciding ahead of time how to use raises can be a key part of the strategy for reaching your financial goals.

Giving

Giving Assets Upon One's Death

"Estate planning is the most fundamental act of stewardship a Christian will ever take." – Dave Keesling, Cofounder of PhilanthroCorp

For many, planning your estate is the largest single act of financial stewardship because we are giving from the largest portion of what we have. For most people a large majority of their net worth involves the equity in their home, life insurance, and various retirement funds.

A will or trust enables you to provide guardianship for minor children, trusteeship over life insurance proceeds and other assets, and in the process:

- Bless your heirs
- Minimize or even eliminate taxes and fees
- Impact your church or other charities you care about

We recommend a three-step process as you consider a will or trust planning.

1. **What do I have?**
    Begin with home equity and stocks, bonds, and other investments. Be sure to include assets such as life insurance, a death benefit, an IRA, or a 401k. There's no need to get an exact value on your stocks or IRA as they fluctuate on a daily basis. It is more important to use an intelligent estimate and to get a will in place as soon as possible. In most cases, you can revise and refine the details of your will or trust at a future date.

2. **Inheritance**
    A helpful guideline for inheritance is to give based on dependency and love. An inheritance will, of course, start with minor children. For young families, much of the inheritance may come from life insurance proceeds. Many insurance professionals suggest ten times your annual income in life insurance as a rule of thumb. This may change as your asset base grows over your lifetime.

    As children become adults your inheritance goals may change based on their needs and maturity.

> > >

A common mistake people make is to think of wills and trusts as a permanent decision. Rather, create a will or trust based on your desired outcome should you die in the next three to five years. At the end of that time, meet with your professionals and take a fresh look based on your current situation and the laws at that time.

3. **Stewardship**

Distribution of our assets upon death includes providing for our minor children or dependent parents, etc., but it can also include gifting to the Lord's work through your local church or other charities. Often this can be done in ways which take advantage of existing tax laws and result in significant charitable giving with only fractional decrease in what is available to heirs.

There are many distribution options to be considered, such as:

1. A percentage of your assets to go to ministries. This could be 10 or 20 percent, or more.

2. An equal portion of your estate to charity and to children. For example, if you have three children, you might divide your estate into four equal parts with one fourth designated to "a child called charity."

3. Capping your children's inheritance with a certain amount going to each child and the balance going to charity.

It has been estimated that less than 30 percent of Americans have a current will (of course, a much higher percentage of Americans will eventually die). Careful planning for the distribution of assets upon our death is the final and perhaps the greatest act of stewardship most of us will have the opportunity to fulfill. Don't miss it!

– Greg Ring, Cofounder of PhilanthroCorp

Saving

The Cumulative Effect of Little Things over an Extended Period

A faucet dripping once a second can release fifty gallons in one week. In the same way, a slow trickle of money can gradually fill financial reservoirs to overflowing or drain them dry. Since everything we have ultimately belongs to God, every financial splash we make can have eternal significance and consequence. To have the financial freedom God intends, we need to learn how to use – rather than be victimized by – the cumulative effect of little things over an extended period.

To get a clearer picture of this important principle – what the Bible has to say about it and how small financial decisions really do add up – consider the Scriptures and examples below.

What the Bible Says

Scripture is clear in its support of the cumulative effect of a little effort over an extended period.

> *Go to the ant, you sluggard; consider its ways and be wise! ... It stores its provisions in summer and gathers its food at harvest.*
> Proverbs 6:6, 8

> *So if you have not been trustworthy in handling worldly wealth, who will trust you with true riches?*
> Luke 16:11

> *Everyone who competes in the games goes into strict training. They do it to get a crown that will not last; but we do it to get a crown that will last forever.*
> 1 Corinthians 9:25

Just a Dollar a Day

The cumulative effect of a little money, just one dollar a day, can be tremendous over a 45-year career depending on whether it is saved or added to debt. The chart below compares saving the dollar in a piggy bank, or a tax-sheltered mutual fund with a 10 percent return, versus charging the dollar to a credit card and incurring a 20 percent interest charge.

> > >

Years	Piggy bank	Invested in a mutual fund with a 10 percent rate of return	Charged to a credit card with a 20 percent interest rate
5	$1,825	$2,329	-$2,957
10	$3,650	$6,080	-$10,316
15	$5,475	$12,121	-$28,626
20	$7,300	$21,849	-$74,190
25	$9,125	$38,751	-$187,566
30	$10,950	$62,752	-$469,681
35	$12,775	$103,391	-$1,171,674
40	$14,600	$168,842	-$2,918,457
45	$16,425	$274,250	-$7,265,012

Major Purchases

The cumulative effect has a great impact on every major purchase. A $20,000 item can cost as little as $17,700 or as much as $25,500 depending on whether we allow the cumulative effect to work for us by saving for it in advance, or against us by incurring debt to purchase now. Consider this example:

To accumulate $20,000 in five years at 5 percent interest, monthly payments to ourselves will have to be $295, and the total of the sixty payments will be $17,700.

To borrow $20,000 for five years at 10 percent interest, monthly payments to the finance company will have to be $425, and the total of the sixty payments will be $25,500.

Start Young

Although students and young adults may not feel they have much in the way of assets, the greatest asset they have is time.

PERSON A - EARLY START
Saving $100 a month during the first 15 years of a career, and then saving nothing more for the next 25 years with a 10 percent return, results in savings of $431,702.

PERSON B - LATE START
Saving nothing during the first 15 years of a career, and then saving $100 a month for the next 25 years with a 10 percent return, results in savings of $123,332.

Note: Person A contributed $18,000; Person B contributed $30,000

Life Expectancy and Replacement Costs of Various Household Items

As can be seen below, both the life expectancy and the cost of household items can vary widely. The use of resources like *Consumer Reports* can be helpful in determining the best balance between cost and quality on many items.

Item	Life Expectancy	Cost to Replace
Appliances		
Dishwasher	5–13 years	$200–$1,000
Dryer	10–25 years	$350–$1,000
Garbage disposal	5–12 years	$70–$300
Microwave oven	9 years	$60–$750
Oven/range	15–20 years	$200–$1,500
Refrigerator	14–19 years	$350–$2,000
Washing machine	10–15 years	$350–$1,000
Cooling		
Central air	10–15 years	$1,800–$3,000
Heat pump	10–15 years	$5,000–$6,000
Window AC unit	10–20 years	$100–$600
Heating		
Forced air furnace	10–25 years	$2,500–$4,500
Plumbing		
Hot water heater	5–15 years	$450–$800
Septic/sewer pump	5–10 years	$1,500–$1,700
Well pump	10 years	$600–$1,200
Roof Covering		
Asphalt standard shingle	12–15 years	$3–$4/sq. foot
Asphalt premium shingle	15–30 years	$4–$6/sq. foot
Wood shingle	10–20 years	$5–$9/sq. foot
Clay tile	20–40 years	$15–$20/sq. foot
Slate tile	40–80 years	$30–$50/sq. foot
Roll roofing	5–15 years	$1–$2/sq. foot

Sources: Association of Home Appliance Manufacturers, Pillar to Post (http://www.pillartopost/home-repair-cost-upgrade-guide.aspx), and Best Buy (http://www.bestbuy.com).

Appendix

The Downside to Taking Loans from Retirement Accounts

The ability to take loans and make "hardship" withdrawals from a company-sponsored retirement plan, such as a 401(k) or 403(b) plan, makes the money in such plans a tempting source of cash. In addition to violating the basic principle that these funds have been set aside for the long-term future, there are significant downsides to borrowing from them.

Borrowing money from your 401(k) or 403(b) plan is allowable by law, but not by every employer. If your employer offers this feature, it usually comes with some limits. For example, you may not be able to borrow more than 50 percent of your vested account balance and only up to a maximum amount – often $50,000.

Disadvantages of borrowing from your retirement plan include:

- Money borrowed from a plan must be repaid with interest.

- Borrowing against your retirement plan reduces the amount that could be earning tax-deferred investment returns for your future. • Repayment must be made within five years. Failure to do so incurs tax and penalty costs. An exception is money borrowed for the purchase of a home, in which case repayment may be extended to 10 or 15 years.

- You'll end up being taxed twice on the money you use to repay your loan, first because money you use to repay the loan is after-tax money, and second because you'll be taxed on the money when you withdraw it in retirement.

- If you leave your employer, you'll need to quickly repay the full amount of your loan – often within 60 days. Otherwise, the loan amount will be considered an early distribution, in which case you will owe taxes and an early withdrawal penalty.

- Under certain circumstances, such as difficulty paying medical bills or your mortgage, you may qualify for a hardship withdrawal from a 401(k) or 403(b) plan. In such cases, the money does not have to be repaid. However, taxes are due along with a 10% penalty – a heavy price to pay in addition to potentially not being prepared for retirement.

Debt
Establishing a Debt Repayment Plan

1. **Establish a Spending Plan based on a temporary, Spartan lifestyle.**
   This frees up every possible dollar for the top priority of debt reduction and establishing an emergency fund.

2. **Determine whether any nonessential assets can be sold.**
   Cash from the sale of assets can be used to give the debt repayment process a kick-start and provide an initial savings buffer to ensure success.

3. **List your debts from smallest to largest.**
   Do not pay attention to the interest rate of the debt.

4. **Pay the current minimum payment on all debts and the maximum additional possible on the smallest. Continue paying the current minimum payments, even if the credit card company lowers the required minimum payment as the principal is reduced.**
   The goal is to pay off smaller debts quickly. This will give a sense of accomplishment as well as simplify the process as the number of creditors is reduced. Although one could argue that the greatest overall savings would occur by paying off the highest interest debt first, the psychological impact of getting some debts paid quickly far exceeds the downside of the few additional interest dollars it may cost. When only debts of relatively the same amount remain to be paid, apply extra payment to the one with the highest interest.

5. **As each debt is paid off, roll the total amount you were paying to the next largest debt.**
   Add that amount to the minimum payment you were making.

6. **Continue this strategy until all debts are paid.**
   Do not reduce the total amount going to debt repayment as some debts are paid off. It is the "snowball" effect of rolling the previous payment into the next largest debt that gives this system its power.

> > >

7. **Incur no new debt, period!**

   Discipline will be necessary in this regard. Obviously, you will not make progress if you are continuing to incur new debt as you are attempting to pay off the old. Be creative. Have someone hold you accountable. Ask for God's help. Know in your heart you are doing the right thing.

8. **Discard credit cards.**

   Get rid of them. If you must have a card for travel or emergency, have only one.

9. **Reward yourself occasionally but modestly.**

   As progress is made and milestones are reached, it is appropriate to reward yourself. For some, the progress itself may be reward enough.

The following page shows a sample Debt Reduction Plan and an explanation for each column. A blank Debt Reduction Plan is included in the Forms section on page 139 and an electronic version, which automatically calculates the pay-off dates, appears on the Good $ense Web site at www.willowcreek.com/freedup.com

Sample Debt Reduction Plan

Item	Amount Owed	Interest	Minimum Monthly Payment	Additional Payment $150	Payment Plan and Pay-off Dates				
					3 Months	6 Months	15 Months	22 Months	26 Months
Sears	$372	18.0	$15	$165	paid!				
Doctor	$550	0	$20	$20	$185	paid!			
Visa	$1980	19.0	$40	$40	$40	$225	paid!		
MasterCard	$2369	16.9	$50	$50	$50	$50	$275	paid!	
Auto	$7200	6.9	$259	$259	$259	$259	$259	$534	paid!
Total	$12,471		$384	$534	$534	$534	$534	$534	0

- The first and second columns list to whom the debt is owed and the amount owed. Debts are listed in the order of lowest to highest amount.
- The third and fourth columns list the interest rate and the minimum monthly payment for each debt.
- The fifth column indicates the amount of additional payment above the minimum that can be made and adds that amount to the minimum payment for the first (smallest) debt listed.
- The remaining columns show how, as each debt is paid, the payment for it is rolled down to the next debt. Pay-off dates can be calculated in advance or simply recorded as they are achieved.

To access an electronic version of this form for your own use, go to www.willowcreek.com/freedup

Appendix

How Extra Payments Can Dramatically Reduce Your Mortgage Debt

Making even modest additional payments to your mortgage can have a significant impact on your pay-off date and the amount of interest you pay. The chart below is based on a $200,000 30-year mortgage at a 7% fixed interest rate. The monthly payments for this loan would be $1,331*. At $100 extra per month, which is just under one extra payment per year, the mortgage would be paid off in 24 years with a savings of more than $63,000 in interest.

Extra Payment	Out of Debt in ...	Total Interest Paid	Interest Saved
$0/month	30 years	$279,022	–
$25/month	28 years	$259,278	$19,744
$50/month	27 years	$242,589	$36,433
$100/month	24 years	$215,709	$63,313

* $1,331 is just for the principal and interest on the loan. Monthly payments usually include an additional amount for taxes and homeowners insurance, as well as private mortgage insurance if there is not a significant down payment.

Spending

When Is Enough, Enough?

The Bible doesn't give absolute guidelines for deciding when enough is enough, but the following nine principles can provide guidance for making wise financial decisions or evaluating a desire to purchase something.

1. Start with the right attitude: everything you have was created by God, is owned by God, and is to be used for God's purposes.

2. If the desire seems reasonable to mature Christian brothers and sisters whose discernment you respect, it is usually wise.

3. If the desire arises from pain over the plight of the poor, the unfortunate, or the disenfranchised, it is likely to be Spirit-led and honoring to God.

4. If the desire involves the well-being of children, it is often right.

5. If the desire is primarily one of wanting to improve your own living conditions or lifestyle, you should not automatically assume it is wrong.

6. Consider whether the desire springs from an incompleteness in your relationship with Christ. Are you trying to fill with purchases an empty place in your heart?

7. Consider whether the resources of God's creation would be adequate to provide for all of His children the thing you desire for yourself.

8. Evaluate how important your desire seems in the context of your own mortality. Ask, "How important will this purchase seem to me when I am on my deathbed?"

9. Ask, "What would Jesus do in my situation?"

Points two through six adapted from *Freedom of Simplicity*, Richard J. Foster (HarperCollins, San Francisco, 1981), pages 88-89. Used by permission.

Appendix

Nothing Down, Nothing a Month

One way products and services are sold is by offering consumers unbelievable financing. Have you ever heard of "90 days same as cash" or "no finance charges until January" or "no-interest financing"? Did it ever occur to you that in a world driven by money markets, a company offering zero interest with no ulterior motive would soon go broke?

Here is how it really works. First, the product is priced higher to cover the expense of the zero-interest financing. So there is actually no savings to begin with. But the story just starts there. Most dealers then sell the financing contract to a finance company to buy. And why would a finance company buy a contract at zero interest? Because the dealer (a furniture store, department store, electronics store, etc.) – who marked the item up in the first place – sells the financing contract to the finance company at a discount. Everyone but the purchaser wins. The dealer got what they wanted – an immediate sale at a regular profit (after the discount to the finance company). And when the buyer pays off the finance company, the finance company makes a profit because they got the buyer's contract at a discount from the dealer.

Second, and more importantly, over 70 percent of the time the buyer does not pay off the dealer within the stated period. Then the finance company gladly begins to charge interest and initiates a longer payment plan. When this occurs, the buyer often pays over 24 percent interest (if that state allows it) and the contract is on prepaid interest or "rule of 78's," which means there is a huge prepayment penalty. Plus, the company will add interest for the original 90 days, which is only "free" if paid off within the 90 days. They also typically will sell overpriced life and disability insurance to pay off their overpriced loan should something happen to your overpriced self. I once met a man who had life insurance on a loan against a rototiller!

This brilliant zero-interest plan now has turned into one of the worst financial decisions ever made because of the total cost of that item. A $1,000 couch at 25 percent for three years with credit life and disability insurance can end up costing at least $1,900.

Adapted from *Financial Peace*, Dave Ramsey (Viking Press, New York, 1992, 1997), pages 39-40. Used by permission.

Resisting the Urge to Purchase

Understanding the forces at work and your particular motivation for buying can be helpful in overcoming the urge to purchase. Is your trip to your favorite store or Web site the result of a spat with your spouse or a particularly large number when you stepped on the scale? Did you just get a raise and feel you absolutely deserve to spend some of it right now? Or, were you feeling lonely and are just so grateful to the solicitous salesperson who seemed to be the first person in a very long time to care about what might make you happy? (Remember, that may be true but it's also part of the salesperson's job.)

Psychologist April Benson, author of *I Shop, Therefore I Am*, gives all her clients a laminated card with six questions on it to put in their wallet on top of their credit cards. She suggests pausing every time you approach the register and asking yourself:

- Why am I here?
- How do I feel?
- Do I need this?
- What if I wait?
- How will I pay for it?
- Where will I put it?

Another helpful approach is to make the commitment to wait 30 days before purchasing that new thing you would like to have. Write it down on a card with the date. If within the 30 day waiting period you find something else you want more than the original thing, write it down, scratch out the original, and begin a new 30 day waiting period. Many have found that in following this process they seldom get to the end of 30 days with a given item. If they do, the above six questions can then be employed as a further check as to the advisability of the purchase.

A Big Difference in a Short Time: Buying a Used Car

Question: I'm determined to be a better steward of God's resources. It would be an encouragement to me if I could do something that would make a big difference in a short time. Do you have a suggestion?

Answer: Except for housing (an expense that may be hard to change), cars are the biggest drain on most budgets. The average price of a new car in the United States is $19,000. Although cars remain reliable for an average of over 13 years and 145,000 miles, Americans tend to keep cars an average of only four years and 55,000 miles. Hanging on to your present car — or buying a good used car instead of a new one — may be the "one big thing" you could do to free up a significant amount of money for higher purposes.

Here are some facts you might consider when you decide whether having an older car is appropriate for you:

- A car loses most of its trade-in value in the first four years. If you trade in a new car after four or fewer years, you're paying a tremendous price for less than one-third the useful life of the car. On the other hand, if you buy a good used vehicle, you can get more than two-thirds of the useful life of the car at a relatively thrifty price.

- We typically assume that new cars are more reliable than used cars. However, according to *Consumer Reports*, cars less than one year old make as many trips to the repair shop as cars that are four or five years old. The most reliable years of a car's life are the second and third years.

- When you select a new car, you have to base your decision on the manufacturer's claims, but used cars have a track record you can check. Most libraries have the annual buying guide published by *Consumer Reports*, which rates used cars and provides repair records for most models. Information is also available on www.consumerreports.org. Also, you can visit the National Highway Traffic Safety Administration Web site (www.nhtsa.gov) or call (800-424-9393) to check if a used car has ever been recalled.

- As a car gets older, the costs for gas and oil increase, but the costs for collision and theft insurance decrease.

- New car dealers typically save the best trade-in cars to sell on their own used car lots. These cars are often thoroughly checked and backed by a used car warranty. In some cases, used car buyers may even inherit the remainder of the manufacturer's new car warranty.

- Recently, leasing has become a popular option and is pushed heavily by many auto dealers. No wonder — it's a good deal for them. The appeal to many unsuspecting folks is the lower monthly payment. Payments should be lower — at the end of the lease you don't own anything! The up-side for used car buyers is that an increasing number of leased cars are being turned in at the end of the lease and then turn up on used car lots.

Bottom Line:

- A comparison of the cost differential of keeping a four-year-old car for another four years and spending more on gas, oil, tires, and maintenance versus buying a new car showed the savings in keeping the four-year-old car to be over $6,000, assuming the new car would be paid for in cash. Add a couple thousand more dollars if it would be financed.

- A comparison of buying a two-year-old used car and keeping it for eight years versus leasing a new car every three years over a "driving lifetime" of forty-eight years revealed a staggering (almost unbelievable) differential of over $400,000.

You might quibble over some of the assumed costs, and the equation might change by some thousands of dollars, but the point is clear — huge savings are possible in the area of automobiles.

When Jesus spoke about avoiding "treasures on earth, where moth and rust destroy and where thieves break in and steal," he could have been speaking of cars. Probably his advice to Christian families today would be "Keep the heap," and "Store up for yourselves treasures in heaven, where moth and rust do not destroy, and where thieves do not break in and steal. For where your treasure is, there your heart will be also" (Matthew 6:20-21).

Information on costs and savings taken from "A Big Difference in a Short Time," by Jon Kopke, College Hill Presbyterian Church Belltower News (November, 1996). Used by permission.

How to Get the Most Out of Every Tank of Gas

- Observe the speed limit.

- Take heavy objects out of your trunk.

- While waiting for a train, or any similar wait of more than a minute or two, turn off the engine.

- Keep your tires properly inflated.

- Keep your engine properly tuned.
  - Change air filters regularly.

- Accelerate slowly and smoothly.

- Combine trips.

- Find someone to share the ride.

- Consider fuel economy when choosing your next vehicle.

Source: www.fueleconomy.gov

Unplugging from the Consumptive Society

It was once said, "There are two ways of getting enough: one is to continue to accumulate more of it, the other is to desire less." Here are ten tips on simplifying life and being a good steward.

1. **Know where your money goes — develop a budget.**
   If we make no more than $40,000 per year for 45 working years, we will have been the stewards of $1,800,000! How dare we consider handling that amount of money without keeping records and knowing where it went! Also, treat the giving portion of your budget differently than your operating budget. The goal of the operating budget is to hold down expenditures, but the goal of giving is to increase expenditures.

2. **Actively reject the advertising industry's persuasive and pervasive attempt to squeeze you into its mold.**
   Greet with sarcastic laughter all the patently false claims of phony TV commercials. Have your family shout in unison, "Who do you think you're kidding?" The goal of advertising is to create a desire for products. This is often done by creating dissatisfaction with what you now have, even though it may be quite satisfactory. Avoid settings that subject you to these overt efforts to create a mindset that is antithetical to Christ's teachings. Don't watch ads on TV. Don't read mail-order catalogs. Don't window shop in malls. Look at advertisements only after you have carefully determined your need for a particular product, and then only to seek the best quality at the lowest price.

3. **When you do decide it is right to purchase an item, see if God will provide it without you having to buy it.**
   Pray about it for a week, then consider if you still need it. If God hasn't provided it and you do still need the item, go ahead and purchase it. This practice integrates our needs with the concept of God's provision and has the additional benefit of avoiding impulse buying.

4. **Stress the quality of life above quantity of life.**
   Refuse to be seduced into defining life in terms of having, rather than being. Learn the wonderful lesson that to increase the quality of life means to decrease material desire — not vice versa.

5. **Make recreation healthy, happy, and gadget free.**
   Consider noncompetitive games — why must there always be a winner? Avoid "spectatoritis." Modern spectator sports programs are obscene in their waste of human and material resources. It is a joy to watch some games, but addiction to doing so is another thing altogether. Develop the habit of homemade celebrations. Read together, play games, tell stories, have skits, invite other families in (and don't kill yourself preparing for them).

> > >

6. **Learn to eat sensibly and sensitively.**

   Eliminate prepackaged dinners. Plan menus ahead, and buy only to meet the menu. Eliminate nonnutritious snack foods. Be conscious of the bio food chain. Grain-fed animals that require ten pounds of grain to produce one pound of meat are a luxury that the bio food chain cannot sustain for the masses of humanity. Get in on the joy of gardening. Dwarf fruit trees can supply large quantities of fresh fruit. Explore food cooperatives. Eat out less and make it a celebration when you do. Go without food one day a month and give the money you save to the poor. Buy less food rather than diet pills!

7. **Learn the difference between significant travel and self-indulgent travel.**

   Give your travel purpose. Travel inexpensively. Become acquainted with people as well as places.

8. **Buy things for their usefulness, not their status.**

   Clothes can be quite presentable but inexpensive. Furniture can be used and refinished. Significant amounts of money can be saved buying good used cars and less expensive models. Are you alone after having raised your family? Consider inviting extended family, a college student, or single young person to live with you.

9. **Learn to enjoy things without owning them.**

   Possession is an obsession in our culture. If we own it, we feel we can control it, and if we control it, we feel it will give us more pleasure. This is an illusion. Enjoy the beauty of the beach without the compulsion to buy a piece of it. Many things can be shared among neighbors and friends. Give some things away just for the freedom it brings.

10. **Teach your children by word and deed about the varied uses of money. Provide clear guidelines about what you consider reasonable and unreasonable expenditures.**

    Culture trains children to desire everything in sight when they enter a store. You do them no favor when you give in to their incessant demands. Get them what they need, not what they want; and in time, they will come to want what they need. Provide children with the experience of a growing self-governance. At a young age, offer them an allowance to give them the experience of saving and giving away, and decide with them how to spend the rest. In time, as their allowances and earning abilities grow, go one-half with them on necessities. Eventually, let them pay for everything themselves. Consider the goal of handling all income and expenses except for food and housing by age sixteen and financial independence, except for college expenses, by age eighteen. Consider approaching the cost of college as the young adult's responsibility, with parents acting as a safety net, as opposed to the cost of college being the parents' responsibility, with the young adult chipping in what they can — a very significant difference in philosophy.

* Adapted from *Celebration of Discipline*, Richard J. Foster, (HarperCollins, San Francisco, 1978, 1988, 1998), pages 78-83. Used by permission.

To Buy or Not to Buy: Deciding to Rent or Purchase a Home

If you rent an apartment you've probably been told that you're throwing money away, that real estate is the best investment you can make, and other bits of conventional wisdom. But home ownership is not necessarily best for everyone. Here are some factors to consider.

How Much Can You Put Down?
Low- and no-down payment mortgages became popular in recent years and helped drive up the percentage of households that own their own home. They also drove up the number of foreclosures.

We encourage you to wait to buy until you can afford to make a 20 percent down payment. With such a down payment you will have proven you are disciplined at saving and you will avoid having to pay private mortgage insurance.

What's Your Credit Score?
Before applying for a mortgage, check your credit report and credit score. Get your free credit report from each of the three main credit bureaus via www.annualcreditreport.com. Then purchase your score via the Web site of Fair Isaac Corporation (www.myfico.com), creator of the most widely used credit score – the FICO score. Order "FICO Standard," which should cost less than $20.

As you can see from the information below, your score has a significant impact on the interest rate you will pay on a mortgage, and the subsequent monthly payment. These figures are based on a $200,000 mortgage taken out on June 18, 2008.

FICO Score	APR	Monthly Payment
760-850	6.170%	$1,221
700-759	6.392%	$1,250
660-699	6.676%	$1,287
620-659	7.486%	$1,397
580-619	9.452%	$1,675
500-579	10.311%	$1,801

If your credit score is below 700, find out why by reviewing your credit reports. There may be errors, which you can fix by contacting the credit bureaus. One of the best ways to raise your credit score is to pay all of your bills on time. Try to get your score above 700 before buying.

> > >

How Much of Your Income Will the Payment Require?

Typically, lenders will approve home loans that require monthly payments for the combination of the mortgage principal, interest, property taxes, and insurance ("PITI") that total no more than 28 percent of a borrower's monthly gross income, or when combined with other debt payments such as credit card balances, vehicle loans, and student loans, 36 percent of monthly gross income. In some cases, lenders will raise those ratios.

However, our recommendation is to hold off on buying a home if you carry a balance on your credit cards. Tacking a home loan onto these other debts makes it very difficult to give generously, save adequately, and live with financial margin. Our further recommendation is to take out a mortgage requiring no more than 25 percent of your monthly gross income for the combination of mortgage principal, interest, taxes, and insurance.

Can You Afford the Total Cost of Home Ownership?

For renters, an appliance that stops working or a leaky pipe means calling the landlord to make (and pay for) the repair. For owners, such problems mean out-of-pocket expenses. There are a lot of costs that come with home ownership – from relatively small expenses such as the annual maintenance of your furnace and air conditioner, to much larger expenses such as the replacement of your home's roof – and lots of other costs in between.

You should factor in at least $100 per month for home maintenance and basic repairs. And, you should consider what might need replacing and begin building savings for such items. If you cannot afford to allocate $100 per month of cash flow to maintenance and basic repairs, and to save for bigger-ticket replacement items each month (as much as $100–$200 per month, depending on what may need replacing and when), you cannot afford to buy a home.

How Long Will You Live There?

A generally accepted rule of thumb is that you need to live in a home you purchase for five to seven years in order to recoup the costs of buying. There are a variety of up-front expenses involved in buying, moving in, and "making the home your own." And there are costs associated with selling. So, if there's a good chance you will need or want to move sooner than that, you may be better off renting.

Additional Resources

Bankrate.com provides a great online assessment to help you determine whether it's best to keep renting or if it makes sense to buy (look for "Renting vs. Buying" under "Calculators"). *The New York Times* (www.nytimes.com) offers a free online calculator that helps compare the costs of renting with the costs of buying (search for "renting vs. buying").

Saving on Utility Expenses

The month-after-month savings on utility costs can be an excellent example of the cumulative effect of little things over an extended period of time. Here are a few ideas for saving on utility expenses.

- Shop around for the best telephone plan.

    - Going a la carte – one company for long-distance, another for local service – may be less expensive than going with a bundle.

    - Compare what you're now paying with what's offered through www.MyRatePlan.com or www.ABTolls.com.

    - Consider VoIP (Voice over Internet Protocol) providers such as Vonage (www.vonage.com).

- Don't pay for directory assistance from your home phone or cell phone.

    - If you have access to a computer, use www.Switchboard.com.

    - If you're calling from a home or cell phone, try 1-800-YELLOWPAGES (1-800-935-5697) or 1-800-GOOG-411.

- Be diligent in minimizing energy and water usage.

    - Turn off lights when not in use.

    - Replace incandescent bulbs with compact flourescents.

    - Set the thermostat higher in summer and lower in winter.

    - Use a programmable thermostat.

    - Be sure weather stripping is in good shape.

    - Conserve water use.

- Check the Energy Star Web site (www.energystar.gov) for lots of ideas on saving on the cost of home energy.

Financial Advantages of Buying a Smaller Home

Persons A and B are both approved for a $180,000 30-year mortgage at 7% interest and have $45,000 as a down payment. Person A decides to buy a home for $225,000 (the maximum they are approved for – $180,000 mortgage plus $45,000 down payment). Person B decides to buy a less expensive home for $175,000 but to put the same amount down ($45,000) and to make the same mortgage payment as person A.

Let's track their experience:

	Person A	Person B
COST OF HOME	$225,000	$175,000
DOWN PAYMENT	45,000	45,000
MORTGAGE	180,000	130,000
MONTHLY PAYMENT	$1,198	$1,198*
AMT. OWED END OF YEAR 5	$169,437	$98,531

*Required payment = $865/month

After 5 years, person B sells his home for $175,000 giving him $76,469 cash (175,000 minus $98,531 owed on his original mortgage). He buys a $225,000 house using the cash as down payment leaving a mortgage of $148,531. He continues to pay $1198/month toward that mortgage even though his required payments are only $988.

After 18 more years (23 years after the purchase of the first house), person B's home is paid off. Person B continues to put $1198/month into a mutual fund returning 10% until year 30.

In year 30, both have their homes paid off but person B also has $143,668 in their mutual fund. You decide: was the five-year wait to get the more expensive home worth it?

Record Keeping

Keeping Year-to-Date Totals on the Spending Record

Often it can be helpful to know how you are doing in various categories not just for the current month but from the beginning of the Spending Plan year.

Lines 4 and 5 on the Spending Record provide that information.

Line 4 carries forward the amount each category was over or under the Spending Record from the month before. If this is done each month, and that figure is added to the over or under figure for the current month, the resulting figure represents the status of that category up to this point in the current budget year. In some cases, it may be of little interest to track certain categories because they never vary from budget, and discipline is exercised in those areas. But consider three categories of variable expenses — groceries, clothes, and going out — that have been tracked in the example on page 126.

This current month groceries were $34 under Spending Plan. A total of $480 was allocated but only $446 was spent. In previous months, a total of $218 (line 4) less than what had been allocated was actually spent. That amount, added to the $34 under for this month, gives a Year-to-Date (YTD) total of $252 under the budget (line 5). The food category is in good shape for the year.

The clothing category is $35 over budget for this month and $142 over for the year at the end of last month. As a result, this category is now $177 over for the year to date.

The going out category is $13 under the allotment for this month but was $96 over the allotment prior to this month. That means this category is $83 over the budget for the year.

This cumulative data can be very helpful as the year progresses. In this situation, if the holiday season were approaching, money would be available in the grocery category to have guests over for some nice holiday meals and still stay within the food budget for the year.

On the other hand, since the clothing category is over budget, it might be a good idea to pass the hint to others that it would be nice to get clothing gifts for Christmas!

Moderation in the "going out" category is also needed in order to bring that Spending Plan category back into budget.

Appendix

Spending Record Example

Daily Variable Expenses

	Transportation		Household						Professional Services	Entertainment		
	Gas, etc.	Maint/Repair	Groceries	Clothes	Gifts	Household Items	Personal	Other		Going Out	Travel	Other
(1) Spending Plan	200	40	480	150	80	75	50	---	---	100	70	40
	64	21	186	89	17	14	16	25		22	70	22 (sitter)
	42		22	46	55	22	18			46		
	38		20	50		9				19		
	58		172			31						
			18									
			8									
			20									
(2) Total	202	21	446	185	72	76	34	25	---	87	70	22
(3) (Over)/Under	(2)	19	34	(35)	8	(1)	16	(25)	---	13	---	18
(4) Last Mo. YTD			218	(142)						(96)		
(5) This Mo. YTD			252	(177)						(83)		

X X X X X X X X X X | 10 | 11 | 12 | 13 | 14 | 15 | 16 | 17 | 18 | 19 | 20 | 21 | 22 | 23 | 24 | 25 | 26 | 27 | 28 | 29 | 30 | 31

- Use this page to record expenses that tend to be daily, variable expenses – often the hardest to control.
- Keep receipts throughout the day and record them at the end of the day.
- Total each category at the end of the month (line 2) and compare to the Spending Plan (line 1). Subtracting line 2 from line 1 gives you an (over) or under the budget figure for that month (line 3).
- To verify that you have made each day's entry, cross out the number at the bottom of the page that corresponds to that day's date.
- Optional: If you wish to monitor your progress as you go through the year, you can keep cumulative totals in lines 4 and 5.

Implementation Issues

More than One Paycheck per Month

Item	Spending Plan ($)	1st Paycheck ($)	2nd Paycheck ($)
✔ Giving	350	175	175
✔ Saving	155		155
✔ Mortgage	1100	1100	
✔ Utilities	180		180
✔ Telephone	55		55
✔ Auto Payment	370		370
✔ Debt Repayment	220		220
Clothes	110		110
Gifts	80		80
Gas	150	75	75
Food	460	230	230
Household Misc.	75	50	25
Entertainment	150	75	75
Misc. Small Exp.	45	45	
Total	**3500**	**1750**	**1750**

✔ = Paid by check or electronic withdrawal

Making a one-time plan for how each paycheck will be allocated and simply referring to it each payday can be a wonderful way to ease the anxiety over questions like "Which bill do I pay now?" and "Do I have enough for food and gas?"

In the above example, the person receives net take-home pay of $3,500 per month and is paid twice a month ($1,750 per pay period). The first column represents the Spending Plan for this family. They give $350 per month, save $155, have a mortgage payment of $1,100, and so on.

Out of the first paycheck, checks are written or electronic withdrawals are made for half of the monthly giving and for the mortgage. The rest of the check is used for half of the allocation for gas, food, entertainment, a portion of household/miscellaneous, and all of the miscellaneous small cash expenditure allocation.

Out of the second paycheck, checks are written or electronic withdrawals are made for the other half of giving, all short-term savings, utilities, telephone, auto payment, and debt repayment. The remainder of that check covers the rest of gas, food, household items, and entertainment.

In developing such a plan, it may be necessary to adjust some payment dates to balance out payments from the two checks. Once the plan has been devised, a copy can be kept with your checkbook or on your computer, and it will eliminate any question about how each paycheck is to be used.

Money Building Up in Certain Categories

Once you begin placing money for certain categories that tend to build up over time into a short-term savings account, the question arises, "I have this savings account, and it has an amount of money in it, but how do I tell how much is for what category?"

The ledger sheet on page 129 shows an example to help answer this question. It is a ledger for a money market fund that contains short-term savings that have accumulated for several budgeting categories.

At the top, there is a description of the four funds into which money is being deposited each payday. In this case, the money is for emergencies, vacations, gifts, and auto repair. Lines 1 through 6 on the form are explained below.

Line 1 is the balance brought forward ($3,500) from the previous year. Based on the activity of that year, $2,100 of that $3,500 belongs to the Emergency account, $500 belongs to the Vacation account, $300 belongs to the Gift account, and $600 belongs to the Auto Repair account.

Lines 2 through 6 show the activity in the fund for the most recent month. On January 8, Dan bought Wendy a birthday gift. He entered $40 in the total balance column with parentheses around it, indicating that it is an amount they need to subtract from the balance because they just spent $40. The $40 was also shown as being spent from the Gift fund.

On January 15, Dan got paid. He deposited $235 to the fund, so $235 is shown under the Total Balance column. Of that $235, $100 was for the Emergency fund, $70 was for the Vacation fund, $30 was for the Gift fund, and $35 was for the Auto Repair fund. They show those four figures under each of those funds. Since this was money being added to the funds, the figures do not have parentheses around them.

On January 17, Joe's Transmission Shop hit them hard with a $500 transmission job. They paid that out of their Auto Repair fund.

On January 25, they bought Sam and Mary a wedding present and recorded a $50 deduction from the total column, and a $50 deduction from the gift column.

On January 30, another paycheck was again distributed among the four categories.

The last line shows end-of-the-month totals based on adding and subtracting the transactions. The fund now has a total of $3,380 distributed as shown.

On page 141 is a blank form on which you can set up your own ledger to track savings.

Wendy and Dan's Money Market Fund for Short-Term Savings

	Date	Description	Total Fund Balance	Fund #1 Emergency	Fund #2 Vacation	Fund #3 Gift	Fund #4 Auto Repair	Fund #5
1	12/31	previous year balance forward	3500	2100	500	300	600	
2	1/8	Wendy's birthday gift	(40)			(40)		
3	1/15	paycheck	235	100	70	30	35	
4	1/17	Joe's Transmission Shop	(500)				(500)	
5	1/25	Sam and Mary's Wedding	(50)			(50)		
6	1/30	Paycheck	235	100	70	30	35	
		End of month total	3380	2300	640	270	170	

Notable Quotes

Financial Faithfulness

- "There is no such thing as being right with God and being wrong with money." – Ben Patterson

Financial Foolishness

- "The poorest man I know is the man who has nothing but money." – John D. Rockefeller

Earning

- "Fact: If you make $50,000 per year, you are in the top .899% of the world's richest individuals and there are 5,946,042,435 people who are poorer than you." – www.globalrichlist.com

Giving

- "Generosity is not something God wants from us. It's something He was for us." – Julie Bullock

Debt

- "When you think no one cares you're alive, try missing a couple of car payments." – Unknown

- "Drive-in banks were established so most of the cars today could see their real owners." – E. Joseph Grossman

- "I will live within my means even if I have to go into debt to do it!" – Unknown

Spending

- "It's the eyes of others that destroys us. If all others were blind, what need would I have for fine clothes, fine house?" – Ben Franklin

- "Consumers are in an endless, hopeless search for happiness through the confiscation of things." – Thomas O'Quinn

- "Civilization: a limitless multiplication of unnecessary necessities." – Mark Twain

- "There is a tendency with all material possessions to obscure the needs they cannot satisfy. A full hand helps us forget an empty heart." – Dallas Willard

- "Give a person everything they want and at that moment, everything will not be everything." – Immanuel Kant

- "If you would make a person happy, add not to their possessions, but subtract from the sum of their desires." – Unknown

Recommended Resources

Books

To purchase any of these resources and to see new recommendations, visit the Good $ense Ministry online store at www.goodsenseministry.com.

Biblical Money Management – Theological Perspective
- *Money, Possessions, and Eternity* by Randy Alcorn (Tyndale House, 2003)
- *Stewards in the Kingdom* by R. Scott Rodin (InterVarsity, 2000)
- *Wealth as Peril and Obligation* by Sondra Ely Wheeler (Wm. B. Eerdmans, 1995)
- *God & Your Stuff* by Wesley Willmer (NavPress, 2002)

Biblical Money Management – Practical/How-To
- *Money, Purpose, Joy* (book and workbook) by Matt Bell (NavPress, 2008)
- *The New Master Your Money* by Ron Blue (Moody, 2004)

Christian Living – More Than Financial Aspects
- *Simplify* by Paul Borthwick (Authentic, 2007)
- *Freedom of Simplicity* by Richard Foster (HarperOne, 2005)
- *When the Game is Over, It All Goes Back in the Box* by John Ortberg (Zondervan, 2007)

Christmas/Holidays
- *Debt-Proof the Holidays* by Mary Hunt (DPL Press, 2007)
- *Hundred Dollar Holiday* by Bill McKibben (Simon & Schuster, 1998)

Culture/Consumerism
- *Consumed* by Benjamin Barber (W. W. Norton, 2008)
- *The Overspent American,* Juliet Schor (HarperCollins, 1998)
- *Maxed Out* by James Scurlock (Scribner, 2007)

Debt
- *Debt-Proof Living* by Mary Hunt (DPL Press, 2005)

Environmental Concerns
- *Serve God, Save the Planet* by J. Matthew Sleeth (Zondervan, 2007)
- *Human Footprint* (DVD) with Elizabeth Vargas (*National Geographic,* 2008)

Estate Planning
- *Splitting Heirs* by Ron Blue (Northfield, 2008)

Family/Marriage
- *Half-Price Living* by Ellie Kay (Moody, 2007)
- *Two Incomes and Still Broke?* by Linda Kelly (Three Rivers, 1998)

Generosity/Giving/Tithing
- *The Treasure Principle* by Randy Alcorn (Multnomah, 2005)
- *40 Day Spiritual Journey to a More Generous Life* by Brian Kluth
- *Fields of Gold* by Andy Stanley (Living Books, 2006)
- *A Revolution in Generosity* edited by Wesley Willmer (chapter by Dick Towner) (Moody, 2008)

Investing
- *Faithful Finances 101* by Gary Moore (Templeton Foundation, 2005)
- *Sound Mind Investing* by Austin Pryor (Sound Mind Investing, 2004)

Kids And Money
- *The Berenstain Bears Think of Those in Need* by Stan and Jan Berenstain (Random House, 1999)
- *Your Kids Can Master Their Money* by Ron and Judy Blue (Focus, 2006)
- *Debt-Proof Your Kids* by Mary Hunt (DPL Press, 2007)
- *The Gift of Nothing* by Patrick McDonnell (Little, Brown Young Readers, 2005)

Poverty
- *Our Day to End Poverty* by Shannon Daley-Harris and Jeffrey Keenan (Berrett-Koehler, 2007)

Practical, Daily Money Management
- *Tiptionary 2* by Mary Hunt (DPL Press, 2007)
- *Living Rich by Spending Smart* by Gregory Karp (FT Press, 2008)
- *Degunking Your Personal Finances* by Shannon Plate (Paraglyph Press, 2005)

Small Group Discussion Guides
- *Money, Purpose, Joy Discussion Guide* by Matt Bell (NavPress, 2008)
- *Giving: Unlocking the Heart of Good Stewardship* by John Ortberg, Laurie Pederson, and Judson Poling (Zondervan, 2000)
- *The Treasure Principle Bible Study* by Randy Alcorn and Brian Smith (Multnomah, 2005)

Social Action/Change
- *Irresistible Revolution* by Shane Claiborne (Zondervan, 2006)
- *Everything Must Change* by Brian McLaren (Thomas Nelson, 2007)
- *Justice in the Burbs* by Will and Lisa Samson (Baker Books, 2007)

Message CDs and Transcripts

These messages may be obtained on www.willowcreek.com or by calling (800) 570-9812.

Title	Speaker	Year	Available Formats
Trust Funding - A Revolution of the Heart (Three-Part Series)	Gene Appel	2008	Transcript, CD, mp3
Celebration of Hope, Part 1: Hungry	Nancy Beach	2008	Transcript, CD, mp3
Full Out: Run with Purpose and Passion, Part 8: Giving, 1 Corinthians 16:1-4	Randy Frazee	2007	Transcript, CD, mp3
How Wise People Build Wealth (Three-Part Series)	Bill Hybels	2007	Transcript, CD, mp3, DVD
Word on the Street, Part 3: His Passionate Focus	Bill Hybels	2006	Transcript, CD
BLING-onomic$ (Four-Part Series)	Gene Appel	2006	Transcript, CD, mp3, DVD
Kingdom Justice: The Manna Principle	Robert Guerrero	2005	Transcript, CD
Flow, Part 8: The Power of Desire, Part 2	John Ortberg	2003	Transcript, CD, mp3
God, We NEED a New Year, Part 4: Surviving a Financial Storm	Bill Hybels	2002	Transcript, mp3
God, We NEED a New Year, Part 5: Living in a New Economic Reality	Bill Hybels	2002	Transcript, mp3
Tools for the New Millennium, Part 3: Calculator-Managing You	Bill Hybels	2000	Transcript
It All Goes Back in the Box	John Ortberg	2000	Transcript, CD, mp3
Money, Sex, and Power: Who Owns What	Bill Hybels	1999	Transcript
Money, Sex, and Power: The Financial Ten Commandments	Bill Hybels	1999	Transcript
Truths that Transform, Part 9: Learn to Be Content in All Circumstances	Bill Hybels	1999	Transcript
Christianity Illustrated, Part 7: A Reward Worth Living For	John Ortberg	1998	Transcript
A Faith That Works, Part 14: Words to the Rich	Bill Hybels	1998	Transcript
Making Sense Out of Money (Four-Part Series)	Bill Hybels	1997	Transcript
Achieving Financial Freedom (Four-Part Series)	Bill Hybels	1996	Transcript
This Is The Life, Part 8: What Jesus Really Taught about Greed	John Ortberg	1995	Transcript
Greatest Sermon in History, Part 16: The Truth About Earthly Treasures	Bill Hybels	1994	Transcript
Values Vital to Our Future, Part 3: The Gift of Giving	Bill Hybels	1991	Transcript

Web Sites

College Funding
- www.savingforcollege.com (Look for "World's Simplest College Calculator".)

Comparison Shopping
- www.dealsofamerica.com
- www.pricegrabber.com
- www.shopping.com
- www.shopzilla.com
- www.mysimon.com
- www.nextag.com
- www.bizrate.com

Coupons/Coupon Codes
- www.couponcabin.com
- www.couponmom.com
- www.couponmountain.com
- www.retailmenot.com
- www.fatwallet.com

Credit Report
- www.annualcreditreport.com
  Get a free copy of your credit report. You are entitled by law to receive one each year from each of the three credit reporting agencies.

  Contact information for each agency:
  Equifax: www.equifax.com
  Experian: www.experian.com
  Trans Union: www.transunion.com

- www.pueblo.gsa.gov (Consumer Credit Handbook that explains how to fix errors on credit reports and what to do if you are turned down for credit.)

Debt
- www.nfcc.org (Find a consumer credit counseling agency near you, 800-388-2227.)
- www.debtorsanonymous.org (Find a Debtors Anonymous group near you.)

Good $ense Ministry
- www.goodsenseministry.com (A wide variety of helpful resources such as a debt reduction calculator and electronic versions of the Spending Plan and the Spending Record.)

> > >

Free Stuff
- www.craigslist.org (Check the "free" section under "for sale.")
- www.freecycle.org

Home Repair
- To learn how to do some repairs and remodeling yourself, go to:
  - www.homedepot.com (Click on "Know-How".)
  - www.lowes.com (Click on "Project & Video Center".)
  - www.thisoldhouse.com

Income Tax
- www.irs.gov (Search for "withholding calculator" and see if you are having too much deducted from your paycheck.)

Insurance
- www.lifehappens.org. (This site, from the Life and Health Insurance Foundation for Education, provides good guidance on how much insurance to buy and answers other questions about life, health, disability, long-term care, and more types of insurance.)
- www.ambest.com (Ratings of various insurance companies.)

Interest Rates on Savings Accounts
- www.bankrate.com
- www.imoneynet.com

Newsletters
- www.moneypurposejoy.com (Good $ense sponsored free eNewsletters designed to further equip and encourage you toward wise, God-honoring uses of money.)
- www.goodsenseministry.com (Monthly eNewsletter particularly aimed at stewardship ministry leaders but helpful for anyone.)

Retirement Planning/Investing
- www.choosetosave.org/ballpark (Calculate how much to save for retirement.)
- www.ssa.gov/pgm/links_retirement.htm (Estimate retirement income.)
- www.themotleyfool.com (Provides advice, information, and how-to's on a wide variety of financial and investment topics.)

Vehicles
- www.edmunds.com (Search for "True cost to own" to see how much various vehicles cost in terms of insurance, maintenance, repairs, and more.)
- www.fueleconomy.gov (Information of various vehicles' fuel economy, tips on getting better gas mileage, how to find the lowest gas prices, and more.)
- www.kbb.com (Kelly Blue Book information on how much vehicles are worth.)

Forms

Included on the following pages are perforated forms you can pull out and use. These include the Debt Reduction Plan, Form for Tracking Short-Term Savings, Envelope Record-Keeping Worksheet, the Spending Plan, three copies of the Spending Record, and an expanded version of the Biblical Financial Principles taught in the course.

If you decide to use the written record-keeping system, these forms can be used for the next two months. Feel free to make photocopies of a blank Spending Record to use for subsequent months.

The Biblical Financial Principles are perforated so you can keep them handy and easily refer to them for the Bible's wisdom concerning the use of money.

Debt Reduction Plan

Item	Amount Owed	Interest	Minimum Monthly Payment	Additional Payment $ ____		Payment Plan and Pay-off Dates			
Total									

- The first and second columns list to whom the debt is owed and the amount owed. Debts are listed in the order of lowest to highest amount.
- The third and fourth columns list the interest rate and the minimum monthly payment for each debt.
- The fifth column indicates the amount of additional payment above the minimum that can be made and adds that amount to the minimum payment for the first (smallest) debt listed.
- The remaining columns show how, as each debt is paid, the payment for it is rolled down to the next debt. Pay-off dates can be calculated in advance or simply recorded as they are achieved.

To access an electronic version of this form for your own use, go to www.willowcreek.com/freedup

Appendix

Month _____

Form for Tracking Short-Term Savings

Date	Description	Total Fund Balance	Fund #1	Fund #2	Fund #3	Fund #4	Fund #5

Appendix

Envelope Record-Keeping Worksheet

Envelopes

The boxes below represent envelopes in which you will place cash for variable expenses each month. For each category, write in the category name (clothing, food, etc.) and the budgeted amount.

Category: _____

$ _____

Category: _____

$ _____

Category: _____

$ _____

Category: _____

$ _____

Category: _____

$ _____

Category: _____

$ _____

Category: _____

$ _____

Category: _____

$ _____

Checks/Automatic Withdrawals

Use the entries below to list the regular monthly expenses that you will pay by check or automatic withdrawal.

Category: _____

$ _____

Category: _____

$ _____

Category: _____

$ _____

Category: _____

$ _____

Category: _____

$ _____

Category: _____

$ _____

Category: _____

$ _____

Category: _____

$ _____

...nding Plan

Earnings/Income Per Month		Totals
Salary #1 (net take-home)	_____	
Salary #2 (net take-home)	_____	
Other (less taxes)	_____	
Total Monthly Income		$ _____

% Guide*

1. Giving		$ _____
Church	_____	
Other Contributions	_____	

2. Savings	15%	$ _____
Emergency	_____	
Replacement	_____	
Long Term	_____	

3. Debt	0-10%	$ _____
Credit Cards:		
Visa	_____	
MasterCard	_____	
Discover	_____	
American Express	_____	
Gas Cards	_____	
Department Stores	_____	
Education Loans	_____	
Other Loans:		
Bank Loans	_____	
Credit Union	_____	
Family/Friends	_____	
Other	_____	

4. Housing	25-36%	$ _____
Mortgage/Taxes/Rent	_____	
Maintenance/Repairs	_____	
Utilities:		
Electric	_____	
Gas	_____	
Water	_____	
Trash	_____	
Telephone/Internet	_____	
Cable TV	_____	
Other	_____	

5. Auto/Transp.	15-20%	$ _____
Car Payments/License	_____	
Gas & Bus/Train/Parking	_____	
Oil/Lube/Maintenance	_____	

6. Insurance (Paid by you)	5%	$ _____
Auto	_____	
Homeowners	_____	
Life	_____	
Medical/Dental	_____	
Other	_____	

7. Household/Personal	15-25%	$ _____
Groceries	_____	
Clothes/Dry Cleaning	_____	
Gifts	_____	
Household Items	_____	
Personal:		
Tobacco & Alcohol	_____	
Cosmetics	_____	
Barber/Beauty	_____	
Other:		
Books/Magazines/Music	_____	
Allowances	_____	
Personal Technology	_____	
Extracurricular Activities	_____	
Education	_____	
Pets	_____	
Miscellaneous	_____	

8. Entertainment	5-10%	$ _____
Going Out:		
Meals	_____	
Movies/Events	_____	
Babysitting	_____	
Travel (Vacation/Trips)	_____	
Other:		
Fitness/Sports	_____	
Hobbies	_____	
Media Rental	_____	
Other	_____	

9. Prof. Services	5-15%	$ _____
Child Care	_____	
Medical/Dental/Prescriptions	_____	
Other:		
Legal	_____	
Counseling	_____	
Professional Dues	_____	

10. Misc. Small Cash Expenditures	2-3%	$ _____
Total Expenses		$ _____

*This is a percent of total monthly income. These are guidelines ...ly and may be different for individual situations. However, there ...ould be good rationale for a significant variance.

TOTAL MONTHLY INCOME	$ _____
LESS TOTAL EXPENSES	$ _____
INCOME OVER/(UNDER) EXPENSES	$ _____

Spending Record

Daily Variable Expenses

	Transportation		Household						Professional Services	Entertainment		
	Gas, etc.	Maint/Repair	Groceries	Clothes	Gifts	Household Items	Personal	Other		Going Out	Travel	Other
(1) Spending Plan												
1												
2												
3												
4												
5												
6												
7												
8												
9												
10												
11												
12												
13												
14												
15												
16												
17												
18												
19												
20												
21												
22												
23												
24												
25												
26												
27												
28												
29												
30												
31												
(2) Total												
(3) (Over)/Under												
(4) Last Mo. YTD												
(5) This Mo. YTD												

- Use this page to record expenses that tend to be daily, variable expenses – often the hardest to control.
- Keep receipts throughout the day and record them at the end of the day.
- Total each category at the end of the month (line 2) and compare to the Spending Plan (line 1). Subtracting line 2 from line 1 gives you an (over) or under the budget figure for that month (line 3).
- To verify that you have made each day's entry, cross out the number at the bottom of the page that corresponds to that day's date.
- Optional: If you wish to monitor your progress as you go through the year, you can keep cumulative totals in lines 4 and 5.

Appendix

Spending Record

Month _____

Monthly Regular Expenses (generally paid by check once a month)

| | Giving | | Savings | Debt | | | Housing | | | | Auto Pmts. | Insurance | | Misc. |
	Church	Other		Credit Cards	Education	Other	Mort/Rent	Maint.	Utilities	Other		Auto/Home	Life/Med.	Cash Exp.
(1) Spending Plan														
(2) Total														
(3) (Over)/Under														
(4) Last Mo. YTD														
(5) This Mo. YTD														

- This page allows you to record major monthly expenses for which you typically write just one or two checks per month.
- Entries can be recorded as the checks are written (preferably) or by referring back to the check ledger at a convenient time.
- Total each category at the end of the month (line 2) and compare to the Spending Plan (line 1). Subtracting line 2 from line 1 gives you an (over) or under the budget figure for that month (line 3).
- Use the "Monthly Assessment" section to reflect on the future actions that will be helpful in staying on course.

Monthly Assessment

Area	(Over)/Under	Reason	Future Action

Areas of Victory _____

Areas to Watch _____

Month _____

Spending Record

Daily Variable Expenses

	Transportation		Household					Professional Services	Entertainment		
	Gas, etc.	Maint/Repair	Groceries	Clothes	Gifts	Household Items	Personal	Other		Going Out	Travel	Other
(1) Spending Plan												
1												
2												
3												
4												
5												
6												
7												
8												
9												
10												
11												
12												
13												
14												
15												
16												
17												
18												
19												
20												
21												
22												
23												
24												
25												
26												
27												
28												
29												
30												
31												
(2) Total												
(3) (Over)/Under												
(4) Last Mo. YTD												
(5) This Mo. YTD												

- Use this page to record expenses that tend to be daily, variable expenses – often the hardest to control.
- Keep receipts throughout the day and record them at the end of the day.
- Total each category at the end of the month (line 2) and compare to the Spending Plan (line 1). Subtracting line 2 from line 1 gives you an (over) or under the budget figure for that month (line 3).
- To verify that you have made each day's entry, cross out the number at the bottom of the page that corresponds to that day's date.
- Optional: If you wish to monitor your progress as you go through the year, you can keep cumulative totals in lines 4 and 5.

Spending Record

Month _____

Monthly Regular Expenses (generally paid by check once a month)

| | Giving | | Savings | Debt | | | Housing | | | | Auto Pmts. | Insurance | | Misc. |
	Church	Other		Credit Cards	Education	Other	Mort/Rent	Maint.	Utilities	Other		Auto/Home	Life/Med.	Cash Exp.
(1) Spending Plan														
(2) Total														
(3) (Over)/Under														
(4) Last Mo. YTD														
(5) This Mo. YTD														

- This page allows you to record major monthly expenses for which you typically write just one or two checks per month.
- Entries can be recorded as the checks are written (preferably) or by referring back to the check ledger at a convenient time.
- Total each category at the end of the month (line 2) and compare to the Spending Plan (line 1). Subtracting line 2 from line 1 gives you an (over) or under the budget figure for that month (line 3).
- Use the "Monthly Assessment" section to reflect on the future actions that will be helpful in staying on course.

Monthly Assessment

Area	(Over)/Under	Reason	Future Action

Areas of Victory _____

Areas to Watch _____

Month _____

Spending Record

Daily Variable Expenses

| | Transportation | | Household | | | | | Professional Services | Entertainment | | |
	Gas, etc.	Maint/Repair	Groceries	Clothes	Gifts	Household Items	Personal	Other		Going Out	Travel	Other
(1) Spending Plan												
(2) Total												
(3) (Over)/Under												
(4) Last Mo. YTD												
(5) This Mo. YTD												

| 1 | 2 | 3 | 4 | 5 | 6 | 7 | 8 | 9 | 10 | 11 | 12 | 13 | 14 | 15 | 16 | 17 | 18 | 19 | 20 | 21 | 22 | 23 | 24 | 25 | 26 | 27 | 28 | 29 | 30 | 31 |

- Use this page to record expenses that tend to be daily, variable expenses – often the hardest to control.
- Keep receipts throughout the day and record them at the end of the day.
- Total each category at the end of the month (line 2) and compare to the Spending Plan (line 1). Subtracting line 2 from line 1 gives you an (over) or under the budget figure for that month (line 3).
- To verify that you have made each day's entry, cross out the number at the bottom of the page that corresponds to that day's date.
- Optional: If you wish to monitor your progress as you go through the year, you can keep cumulative totals in lines 4 and 5.

Appendix

Month _____

Spending Record

Monthly Regular Expenses (generally paid by check once a month)

| | Giving | | Savings | Debt | | | | Housing | | | | Auto Pmts. | Insurance | | Misc. |
	Church	Other		Credit Cards	Education	Other		Mort/Rent	Maint.	Utilities	Other		Auto/Home	Life/Med.	Cash Exp.
(1) Spending Plan															
(2) Total															
(3) (Over)/Under															
(4) Last Mo. YTD															
(5) This Mo. YTD															

- This page allows you to record major monthly expenses for which you typically write just one or two checks per month.
- Entries can be recorded as the checks are written (preferably) or by referring back to the check ledger at a convenient time.
- Total each category at the end of the month (line 2) and compare to the Spending Plan (line 1). Subtracting line 2 from line 1 gives you an (over) or under the budget figure for that month (line 3).
- Use the "Monthly Assessment" section to reflect on the future actions that will be helpful in staying on course.

Monthly Assessment

Area	(Over)/Under	Reason	Future Action

Areas of Victory _____

Areas to Watch _____

Biblical Financial Principles

FOUNDATION OF THE GOOD $ENSE MINISTRY
Cultivate a steward's mindset.

GOD CREATED EVERYTHING
In the beginning there was nothing, and God created (Genesis 1:1).

GOD OWNS EVERYTHING
"The silver is mine and the gold is mine,' declares the LORD Almighty" (Haggai 2:8). "Every animal of the forest is mine, and the cattle on a thousand hills" (Psalm 50:10). "The earth is the LORD's, and everything in it, the world, and all who live in it" (Psalm 24:1).

Flowing out of the fact that God created and owns everything is the logical conclusion that whatever we possess is not really ours, but belongs to God; we are trustees, not owners. Therefore, we are trustees, not owners. Although 1 Corinthians 4 (quoted below) does not directly refer to material possessions, its counsel is applicable to this aspect of life as well.

WE ARE TRUSTEES
"A person who is put in charge as a manager must be faithful" (1 Corinthians 4:2, NLT).

WE CANT SERVE TWO MASTERS
"No one can serve two masters. For you will hate one and love the other; you will be devoted to one and despise the other. You cannot serve both God and money" (Matthew 6:24, NLT).

USE RESOURCES WISELY
"His master replied, 'Well done, good and faithful servant! You have been faithful with a few things; I will put you in charge of many things. Come and share your master's happiness!'" (Matthew 25:21).

PURSUE BIBLICAL FINANCIAL KNOWLEDGE
"Buy the truth and do not sell it; get wisdom, discipline and understanding" (Proverbs 23:23). "Plans fail for lack of counsel, but with many advisers they succeed" (Proverbs 15:22).

MEASURABLE GOALS AND REALISTIC PLANS
"Commit to the LORD whatever you do, and your plans will succeed" (Proverbs 16:3).

TRUSTWORTHINESS MATTERS
"Whoever can be trusted with very little can also be trusted with much, and whoever is dishonest with very little will also be dishonest with much. So if you have not been trustworthy in handling worldly wealth, who will trust you with true riches? And if you have not been trustworthy with someone else's property, who will give you property of your own?" (Luke 16:10–12).

EARNING
The Diligent Earner – One who produces with diligence and purpose and is content and grateful for what he or she has.

God established work while Adam and Eve were yet in the Garden of Eden. God invited them to join him in the ongoing act of caring for creation. Work came before the fall of Adam and Eve and is a blessing, not a curse. All work has dignity. Our work should be characterized by the following principles.

BE DILIGENT; SERVE GOD
"Whatever you do, work at it with all your heart, as working for the Lord" (Colossians 3:23).

PROVIDE FOR OURSELVES AND THOSE DEPENDENT ON US
"Those who won't care for their relatives, especially those in their own household, have denied the true faith. Such people are worse than unbelievers" (1 Timothy 5:8).

BE GRATEFUL; REMEMBER FROM WHOM INCOME REALLY COMES
"Remember the LORD your God, for it is he who gives you the ability to produce wealth" (Deuteronomy 8:18).

ENJOY YOUR WORK; BE CONTENT IN IT
"…It is good for people to eat, drink, and enjoy their work under the sun during the short life God has given them, and to accept their lot in life. And it is a good thing to receive wealth from God and the good health to enjoy it. To enjoy your work and accept your lot in life – this is indeed a gift from God" (Ecclesiastes 5:18-19 NLT).

BE TRANSFORMED WORKERS
"Slaves, obey your earthly masters with respect and fear, and with sincerity of heart, just as you would obey Christ. Obey them not only to win their favor when their eye is on you, but like slaves of Christ, doing the will of God from your heart" (Ephesians 6:5-6).

EARN POTENTIAL, SHARE EXCESS
"If you are a thief, quit stealing. Instead, use your hands for good, hard work, and then give generously to others in need" (Ephesians 4:28 NLT).

GIVING
The Generous Giver – One who gives with an obedient will, a joyful attitude, and a compassionate heart.

WE ARE MADE TO GIVE
We are made in the image of God (Genesis 1:26-27). God is gracious and generous. We will lead a more satisfied and fulfilled life when we give to others.

GIVE AS A RESPONSE TO GOD'S GOODNESS
"Every good and perfect gift is from above…" (James 1:17). Therefore, we give out of gratefulness for what we have received.

GIVE TO FOCUS ON GOD AS OUR SOURCE AND SECURITY
"But seek first his kingdom and his righteousness and all these things will be given to you as well" (Matthew 6:33).

GIVE TO HELP ACHIEVE ECONOMIC JUSTICE
"Our desire is … that there might be equality. At the present time your plenty will supply what they need" (2 Corinthians 8:13-14). Throughout Scripture, God expresses his concern for the poor and calls us to share with those less fortunate.

GIVE TO BLESS OTHERS
"I will make you into a great nation and I will bless you; I will make your name great, and you will be a blessing." (Genesis 12:2). If we are blessed with resources beyond our needs, it is not for the purpose of living more lavishly but to bless others. We are blessed to be a blessing.

BE WILLING TO SHARE
"Command them [the rich] to do good, to be rich in good deeds, and to be generous and willing to share" (1 Timothy 6:18).

GIVE TO BREAK THE HOLD OF MONEY
Another reason to give is that doing so breaks the hold that money might otherwise have on us. While the Bible doesn't specifically say so, it is evident that persons who give freely and generously are not controlled by money but have freedom.

GIVE JOYFULLY, GENEROUSLY, IN A TIMELY MANNER
"Out of the most severe trial, their overflowing joy and their extreme poverty welled up in rich generosity. For I testify that they gave as much as they were able, and even beyond their ability. Entirely on their own, they urgently pleaded with us for the privilege of sharing in this service to the saints" (2 Corinthians 8:2-4).

GIVE WISELY
"We want to avoid any criticism of the way we administer this liberal gift" (2 Corinthians 8:20).

GIVE EXPECTANTLY AND CHEERFULLY
"…The one who plants generously will get a generous crop. You must each decide in your heart how much to give. And don't give reluctantly or in response to pressure. For God loves a person who gives cheerfully" (2 Corinthians 9:6-7 NLT; see also verses 10-14).

MOTIVES FOR GIVING ARE IMPORTANT

Unless our motives are right, we can give all we have – even our bodies as sacrifices – and it will be for naught (I Cor. 13). We can be scrupulous with tithing and still not have the right motives. Jesus rebuked the religious leaders of his day for this very thing: "…You hypocrites! You give a tenth of your spices – mint, dill and cumin. But you have neglected the more important matters of the law – justice, mercy and faithfulness" (Matthew 23:23).

SAVING

The Wise Saver – One who builds, preserves, and invests with discernment.

IT IS WISE TO SAVE

"The wise store up choice food and oil, but fools gulp theirs down." (Proverbs 21:20 TNIV). "Go to the ant, you sluggard; consider its ways and be wise! It has no commander, no overseer or ruler, yet it stores its provisions in summer and gathers it food at harvest" (Proverbs 6:6-8).

IT IS SINFUL TO HOARD

"Then he told them a story: 'A rich man had a fertile farm that produced fine crops. He said to himself, "What should I do? I don't have room for all my crops." Then he said, "I know! I'll tear down my barns and build bigger ones. Then I'll have room enough to store all my wheat and other goods. And I'll sit back and say to myself, 'My friend, you have enough stored away for years to come. Now take it easy! Eat, drink, and be merry!'" But God said to him, "You fool! You will die this very night. Then who will get everything you worked for?" Yes, a person is a fool to store up earthly wealth but not have a rich relationship with God'" (Luke 12:16-21 NLT).

CALCULATE COST; PRIORITIZE

"But don't begin until you count the cost. For who would begin construction of a building without first calculating the cost to see if there is enough money to finish it? Otherwise, you might complete only the foundation before running out of money, and then everyone would laugh at you. They would say, 'There's the person who started that building and couldn't afford to finish it!'" (Luke14:28-30 NLT).

AVOID GET-RICH-QUICK SCHEMES

"The trustworthy person will get a rich reward, but a person who wants quick riches will get into trouble" (Proverbs 28:20 NLT).

SEEK WISE COUNSELORS

"Let the wise listen and add to their learning, and let the discerning get guidance" (Proverbs 1:5).

ESTABLISH A JOB BEFORE BUYING HOME

"Finish your outdoor work and get your fields ready; after that, build your house" (Proverbs 24:27).

DIVERSIFY YOUR HOLDINGS

"Give portions to seven, yes to eight, for you do not know what disaster may come upon the land" (Eccles. 11:2).

DEBT

The Cautious Debtor – One who avoids entering into debt, is careful and strategic when incurring debt, and always repays debt.

REPAY DEBT AND DO SO PROMPTLY

"The wicked borrow and do not repay, but the righteous give generously" (Psalm 37:21). "Do not say to your neighbor, 'Come back later; I'll give it tomorrow' – when you now have it with you" (Proverbs 3:28).

AVOID THE BONDAGE OF DEBT

"The rich rule over the poor, and the borrower is servant to the lender" (Proverbs 22:7).

DEBT PRESUMES ON THE FUTURE

"Now listen, you who say, 'Today or tomorrow we will go to this or that city, spend a year there, carry on business and make money.' Why, you do not even know what will happen tomorrow. What is your life? You are a mist that appears for a little while and then vanishes" (James 4:13-14).

DEBT CAN DENY GOD THE OPPORTUNITY TO WORK IN OUR LIVES AND TEACH US VALUABLE LESSONS

God may wish to show us his love by providing us with something we desire but for which we have no resources. If we go into debt to get it anyway, we deny him that opportunity (see Luke 12:22-32). In the same way that parents refrain from giving a child everything the child wants because parents know it isn't in the child's best interest, incurring debt can rob God of the opportunity to teach us through denial. Ecclesiastes 7:14 reminds us: "When times are good, be happy; but when times are bad, consider: God has made the one as well as the other."

DEBT CAN FOSTER ENVY AND GREED

"Beware! Guard against every kind of greed. Life is not measured by how much you own" (Luke 12:15 NLT).

GIVE AND PAY WHAT YOU OWE

"Give to everyone what you owe them: Pay your taxes and government fees to those who collect them, and give respect and honor to those who are in authority" (Romans 13:7 NLT).

DON'T CO-SIGN

"Don't agree to guarantee another person's debt or put up security for someone else. If you can't pay it, even your bed will be snatched from under you" (Proverbs 22:26-27 NLT).

DEBT CAN DISRUPT SPIRITUAL GROWTH

"The fruit of the Spirit is love, joy, peace, patience, kindness, goodness, faithfulness, gentleness and self-control. Against such things there is no law" (Galatians 5:22-23).

SPENDING

The Prudent Consumer – One who enjoys the fruits of their labor yet guards against materialism.

BEWARE OF IDOLS

"You shall not make for yourself an idol in the form of anything in heaven above or on the earth beneath or in the waters below" (Deuteronomy 5:8). Materialism – which so saturates our culture – is nothing less than a competing theology in which matter (things) is of ultimate significance; that is, things become gods or idols. "They …worshiped and served created things rather than the Creator" (Romans 1:25).

GUARD AGAINST GREED; THINGS DO NOT BRING HAPPINESS

"…Beware! Guard against every kind of greed. Life is not measured by how much you own" (Luke 12:15, NLT).

SEEK MODERATION

"…Give me neither poverty nor riches, but give me only my daily bread. Otherwise, I may have too much and disown you and say, 'Who is the LORD?' Or I may become poor and steal, and so dishonor the name of my God" (Proverbs 30:8-9).

BE CONTENT

"I know what it is to be in need, and I know what it is to have plenty. I have learned the secret of being content in any and every situation, whether well fed or hungry, whether living in plenty or in want. I can do everything through him who gives me strength" (Philippians 4:12-13).

"…Godliness with contentment is great gain. For we brought nothing into the world, and we can take nothing out of it. But if we have food and clothing, we will be content with that" (1 Timothy 6:6-8).

DON'T WASTE GOD'S RESOURCES

"When they had all had enough to eat, he said to his disciples, 'Gather the pieces that are left over. Let nothing be wasted'" (John 6:12).

ENJOY A PORTION OF GOD'S PROVISION

"Command those who are rich in this present world not to be arrogant nor to put their hope in wealth, which is so uncertain, but to put their hope in God, who richly provides us with everything for our enjoyment. Command them to do good, to be rich in good deeds, and to be generous and willing to share. In this way they will lay up treasure for themselves as a firm foundation for the coming age, so that they may take hold of the life that is truly life" (1 Timothy 6:17-19).

WATCH YOUR FINANCES (BUDGET)

"Be sure you know the condition of your flocks, give careful attention to your herds; for riches do not endure forever, and a crown is not secure for all generations" (Proverbs 27:23-24).

Notes:

Willow Creek Association

Vision, Training, Resources for Prevailing Churches

This resource was created to serve you and to help you build a local church that prevails. It is just one of many ministry tools that are part of the Willow Creek Resources® line, published by the Willow Creek Association (WCA).

The WCA was created in 1992 to serve a rapidly growing number of churches from across the denominational spectrum that are committed to helping unchurched people become fully devoted followers of Christ. Membership in the WCA now numbers 12,000+ Member Churches worldwide from more than 90 denominations.

The Willow Creek Association links like-minded Christian leaders with each other and with strategic vision, training, and resources in order to help them build prevailing churches designed to reach their redemptive potential. Here are some ways that the WCA does that.

- **Ministry-Specific Conferences** — Throughout the year the WCA hosts a variety of conferences and training events — both at Willow Creek's main campus and offsite, across the U.S., and around the world — targeting church leaders and volunteers in ministry-specific areas such as: group life, preaching and teaching, the arts, children's ministry, student ministry, stewardship, etc.

- **The Leadership Summit** — A once a year, two-day learning experience to envision and equip Christians with leadership gifts and responsibilities. Presented live on Willow's campus as well as via satellite simulcast to 135+ locations across North America — plus more than 80 international cities featuring the Summit by videocast every fall — this event is designed to increase the leadership effectiveness of pastors, ministry staff, volunteer church leaders, and Christians in the marketplace.

- **Willow Creek Resources**® — Provides churches with trusted and field-tested ministry resources in such important topics as leadership, evangelism, group life, spiritual formation, spiritual gifts, stewardship, volunteerism, student ministry, children's ministry, the arts (drama, media, contemporary music), and more.

- **WCA Member Benefits** — Includes substantial discounts to WCA training events, a 20 percent discount on all Willow Creek Resources®, *Defining Moments* monthly audio journal for leaders, quarterly *Willow* magazine, access to a Members-Only section on willowcreek.com, monthly communications, and more. Member Churches also receive special discounts and premier services through WCA's growing number of ministry partners — Select Service Providers — and save an average of $500 annually depending on the level of engagement.

For specific information about WCA conferences, resources, membership, and other ministry services contact:

Willow Creek Association
P.O Box 3188
Barrington, IL 60011-3188

Phone: 800-570-9812
Fax: 847-765-5046
www.willowcreek.com

Take the Next Step in Your Journey Toward Financial Freedom and Joy.

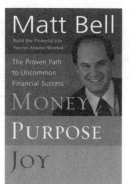

Money, Purpose, Joy
Matt Bell

978-1-60006-279-7
1-60006-279-2

Discover the connection between money and what really matters in life. Financial expert Matt Bell says many of us have settled for far too little in our financial choices. In this helpful and motivating book, he shows how to redirect your use of money to meet your deepest longings.

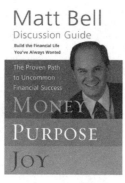

Money, Purpose, Joy: Discussion Guide
Matt Bell

978-1-60006-322-0
1-60006-322-5

Utilize the life-changing environment of a small group to spur each other on toward the financial lives you've always wanted.

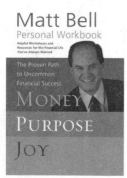

Money, Purpose, Joy: Personal Workbook
Matt Bell

978-1-60006-321-3
1-60006-321-7

The companion workbook provides worksheets, forms, and additional resources to help you build the financial life you've always wanted.

To order copies, call NavPress at 1-800-366-7788.